LANDMARKS OF CONTEMPORARY DRAMA

LANDMARKS OF
CONTEMPORARY DRAMA

By

J. CHIARI, D.ès.L.

LONDON: HERBERT JENKINS

First published by
Herbert Jenkins Limited
3 Duke of York Street
London, S.W.1
1965

MADE AND PRINTED IN GREAT BRITAIN BY
WILLIAM CLOWES AND SONS, LIMITED
LONDON AND BECCLES

CONTENTS

A Joie qui s'y retrouvera

INTRODUCTION

WORDS are slippery coins, difficult to handle; concepts are
fluid, subject to argument, so it might be helpful to make clear
at the outset what certain words and concepts are supposed to
mean. This might at least preclude semantic searches and
narrow the disagreement to acceptance or refusal of the professed meaning. Contemporary drama is supposed to mean in
this study the living drama, that is to say the drama which is
being performed now or has been performed since the end of
the last war. Most of the authors of this living drama are alive
now. Three are no longer so; yet the reasons why they are an
integral part of the living theatre are easy to grasp and practically incontrovertible. Some of O'Neill's plays, including two
of his best, were only performed during the last fifteen years;
Claudel's dramatic fame is above all a post-war phenomenon,
and Brecht, the most radio-active fount of drama at this
moment, falls within the same category.

There have already been many very adequate full-length
studies of most writers discussed in the present work and of the
period under examination. The aim of this study is not to try
to duplicate any of them, but to attempt to single out and to
delineate the main aspects of this living drama and to relate
them to one another and to the tree of western civilisation to
which they belong. A tree is a living, organic thing; art is the
same; so the description of a bright or sere leaf might lead to
references to a bough, branch or stem, but these will never be
any more than guiding signs.

All criticism is, like all human activities, something subjective. Discriminatory criticism aiming at appraising the importance or the non-importance of certain aspects of art is
necessarily more subjective than descriptive or phenomeno-

9

logical criticism. Any rational exploration and exposition of any given problem presupposes beliefs which necessarily play a part in the orientation of these relatively objective pursuits. The hope of any search for religious, artistic or scientific truth is, of course, that the beliefs underlying such a search should be rational. I believe that art is discovery of truth embodied in a symbolic equivalence of experience. I believe that photographic reproductions and imitations of life are always lifeless; life always remains embedded in the original and cannot be conveyed through a photograph of its phenomenal appearance; it can only be intuited through the essential music which makes this appearance. Photographic naturalism can only catch the shadow of a substance which pertains, not to the world of the senses, but to that of the imagination. That is why, meticulous concentrations on details and naturalistic descriptions of circumscribed sections of society, do not, cannot, amount to a living thing, and they generally imply non-aesthetic ends.

This study begins with an examination of the climate of the arts at this moment, with specific reference to nihilism and the absurd. Then comes a brief exposition of the various, present aspects of drama, from tragedy to naturalistic, poetic and prose drama. This is followed by a chapter on the main traits of the work of Sartre, Anouilh, Claudel, Ionesco, Adamov and Beckett. The next chapter deals with the poetic drama of T. S. Eliot and Fry, and is followed by a chapter dealing with the contribution made by the works of Osborne, Wesker, Pinter, Whiting and John Arden. Then comes a chapter dealing with O'Neill's last plays and with the work of Tennessee Williams, Arthur Miller and Edward Albee, then a chapter on the dramatic theories and the work of Berthold Brecht, followed by a chapter on German-speaking drama after Brecht. Finally a few concluding remarks on naturalism, social realism and poetic speech in the theatre now.

CHAPTER ONE

THE CLIMATE OF CONTEMPORARY ART

In our world dominated by journalism, catch-penny phrases, quick generalisations and easy categorisations, writers and artists have no sooner produced two or three works than they are given a label, parcelled up into groups, and have their work thoroughly examined in searching and detailed studies. Generations are now shortened into decades and half decades, and wide-embracing labels are the fashion. Camus's laurels and wide influence have caused much emulation which he himself would certainly have disclaimed. Two of the notions to which he gave wide currency, without any real logical grounding, have caught on with disastrous effect. One is the notion of revolt; the other is that of the absurdity of existence. Both these notions were expounded in *L'homme Révolté* and *Le Mythe de Sisyphe*, two works which illustrate all too clearly Camus's fundamental flaws as a thinker. He certainly was a thoughtful, sincere and profoundly gifted writer, but his thinking is above all affective thinking; his genuine emotions and beliefs, his passionate love of human kind, together with the splendid imagination which gave wings to his words, cause him to leap over logical links and to sweep on right to the end of the sentence without making always sure that it really holds logically together. Sartre was quite justified to criticise the shaky philosophical foundations of *L'homme Révolté; Le Mythe de Sisyphe* suffers from similar weaknesses; yet the notion of the absurd which it expounds has caught like wild-fire, and now it seems, according to certain critics, to embrace the whole world and to cast its roots right back to Shakespeare and even to Sophocles. Yet the notion of the total absurdity of life in a world in which there are hundreds of millions of Christians of all denominations, together with hundreds of millions of Buddhists and of Mahomedans, that is to say, more than half the whole population of the world professing religious beliefs which ascribe both order and finality to life, is obviously untenable. To talk about the world as being absurd is to compare it mentally to an imaginary, rational world, endowed with logic and finality. Such a world can only exist as a concept of the mind of the one who believes in it; yet, without the notion of a perfectly rational world, the notion of an absurd world is unthinkable. The absurd is an historical and changing notion, and "History", as Marx said, "does nothing; it is man, living man, who does everything." It is man who decides whether history is absurd or meaningful. For a people who live in bondage and dejection, history is absurd; but it is not so for people who pursue in freedom and peace, the fulfilment of their humanity and consciousness. The savagery and the cruelty of the Nazis were absurd; the courage and sacrifice of those who resisted them prove man's noble faith in himself and cannot be described as absurd. Those who talk of the absurd in general terms can only do so by ascribing the absurdity of the world to an absent, repudiated or buried God—something which is both hollow rhetoric and a contradiction in terms, as far as the notion of God is concerned. The slum dweller, the poor, the starving and disease-ridden outcasts of the world do not blame their suffering and alienated state on the absurd, but on the society to which they belong, that is to say, on other men who make or unmake the absurd as well as inhumanity and injustice. The world is what men make it. "Objects", says Husserl, "exist for me, and are for me, what they are, only as objects of actual and possible consciousness."*

A much-quoted sentence from Camus illustrates the erroneous ways by which man extricates himself from his responsibility to the world and makes of absurdity, his choice which he accepts with courage. It no doubt sounds noble but it rests on very shaky premises. Here is the sentence: "A world that can be explained by reasoning, however faulty, is a familiar world. But in a universe in which he is suddenly deprived of illusions and light, man feels an exile. This exile is entirely without

* *Cartesian Meditations*, p. 65. Nijhoff, The Hague, 1960.

hope, for he is deprived of the memories of a lost homeland and of the prospects of a promised land. This divorce between man and his life, the actor and his setting truly constitutes the feeling of absurdity" (*Le Mythe de Sisyphe*, p. 18). This is just what Flaubert described disdainfully as "littérature" and Verlaine as "éloquence". It is criss-crossed with pathetic fallacies, romantic wistfulness and incoherence. The sleight of hand, "however faulty", applied to "reasoning", reduces meaning to the euphoric acceptance of a given notion, and not to rationality; for any reasoning which is faulty does not explain; it merely muddles up the mind. Yet this is a very slight point compared with what follows. Who indeed has deprived man of "illusions and light", and why illusions? Was it some supernatural force or was it man himself? Either way, he is bound to be responsible. The first alternative is obviously an allusion to the Nietzschean death of God. But how can man know that God has died, unless he has killed Him in himself, for he could not kill Him any other way? What follows is Werther and Manfred over again, with less guts and less daemonic pride. Man is an exile, says Camus, but who has exiled him? The bad God, no doubt! Therefore there was, there must have been, a God. And how can man be deprived of memories of his lost Eden and of hope of a promised land? Poor, meek and mild child—man frightfully done down by His father—God and divorced from "his life" which becomes a mere stage setting!

Now the image is no doubt fetching, but what in truth is man without life? No wonder the sentence ends with the cry of "absurdity"! God, or the notion of God, is here shadowily used as a stage prop to brush up a scene in which man is back again by the closing gates of Eden with a much fiercer archangel than the one who chased Adam and Eve out of God's pastures, since this one has even brain-washed them of their pleasant memories and illusions. No, the absurdists obviously cannot have their cake and eat it. If God is, He cannot be dismissed as Pascal said about Descartes, with a "chiquenaude", as if He were a useless prompter or a watch-maker who has done his job and can therefore be packed away into limbo. There is no possible limbo without the notion of pure Being or God, and the notion of

God, once accepted, is not something which can be terminated at man's bidding, even if this man is called Nietzsche. There cannot be any "has been" for God. In the fifth century B.C., Parmenides already knew that whatever is, is now and always, without beginning or end, one and all-embracing. If God has been, He is and will always be, if not, it is not God but a figure of speech, a phantom in a nursery which can be used according to the child's needs and fears.

If the world is described by some as absurd, it is men who have made it so and think it so, and men will not change the absurdity of the world by wilfully trying to conform to it and by adopting absurdity as a mode of living. Neither are things neutral, as the novelists of the *nouvelle vague* in France would have it. Whether organic or inorganic, matter is not inanimate, it is alive, orientated towards being and endowed with properties of repulsion and attraction. It is an integral part of creation which comprises man and, as such, it constantly interacts upon him and is interacted upon by him. The phenomenal world is part of man's life and as such it could never be fixed into an immutable appearance, valid for all men at all times; its appearance, or the apprehension of its appearance, is as varied and changing as human life. The most uncompromising phenomenalism, intent upon confining things to their appearances, is always coloured by the apprehending consciousness which is always subjective, even when it professes to be objective.

Sartre is much wiser when he asserts that the world of things is the world of *l'en-soi*, which man can mould according to the workings of his freedom. The absurdity which he descries around him is social, historical and temporal, but neither immanent nor transcendental, two notions which for him are meaningless. He is at least logical, while other atheists are not so, for they merely use the concept of absurdity as a pure and simple romantic device in order to explain the isolation, plight, anxiety and partial incapacity of individuals to communicate with one another and to lead more or less coherent lives. In our time, reason is either blindly worshipped by the devotees of science, or fully distrusted and despised by the absurdists who assert that the world is absurd and that it can only be appre-

14

hended in terms of expressionism, concrete experiences or in-coherent fantasies, in an atmosphere reminiscent of the climate of a ghost train. Absurdity thus becomes a set of jingling bells placed on men's necks so as to deafen them and to goad them on. with stiff upper lip, stoic heart and eyes shut, towards the abyss which they will nobly face. If they dared to open their eyes and to look around them, they would of course see that there is no abyss, except in themselves.

The absurdists who assert that life is absurd know that they themselves are part of the causality of life, and they know also that if they chose to leave it through wilful suicide, they would, by such a choice, assert a belief in rationality which would deny the absurdity which they posit. If life were totally absurd, there could be neither better nor worse; one could only live it as absurd, and to live the absurd is in itself an impossibility, though of course one can indulge the notion of the absurd or live a partially absurd life; but these attitudes rest on subjective beliefs and not on objectivity. Nietzsche's notion of heroic death and Camus's notion of a noble life, in the face of absurdity, are not possible, for the absurd leaves no scope whatever for human freedom. Man can only exercise his freedom in a world which he makes, through his freedom. This is Sartre's position according to whom, living the absurd signifies living in bad faith, that is to say, misusing one's own freedom, and being therefore responsible for what happens in the world. Sartre's notion of freedom as something which is inherent to man and which therefore comes very close to Christian essentialism as expounded by St. Augustin, and to the Kantian intuitive awareness of the true moral choice, is, with the exception of its premises, a more logical and nobler concept than that of any of the absurdists.

The absurd is a relative notion, and not an absolute, and the only notion of the absurd which is possible is that which posits the absurdity of life within the context of transcendence, whether it is that of Pascal and Kierkegaard, with their *Angst* caused by the absence of a living faith in God, or that of Nietzsche for whom God's death had left a terrifying, all-embracing nothingness. The climate of Nietzsche's atheism is profoundly religious and Christian in spite of his longing for presocratic Gods. Nietzsche, the author of *Ecce Homo*, the one who often signed himself "Crucifixus", was, like Kierkegaard and Pascal to whom he owes so much, profoundly pervaded with Christianity which he violently rejected; although of course, he did not reject the idea of a pure Being which he sought in the will to power and in the superhuman. Obsessed with Christ, he tried to make himself Anti-Christ, but he acknowledged the fact that: "Christ on the cross remains the most sublime of all symbols." He replaced transcendence by the immanence of his eternal cycles caught between non-Being and Being to whom he delivered a death certificate. Kierkegaard's Christianity was an absurd paradox, the acceptance of which implied the rejection of the world and the acceptance of martyrdom. Reason was, like Pascalian reason, unable to reach the core of Christianity, thence the leap into faith as lived experience. Few men can claim to have known better than Pascal the power of reason, yet, when it came to using it as a means to reach the truth of Being, he distrusted it as much as Kierkegaard and Nietzsche who crystallise in their respective worlds, the shift from objective to existential thinking and are the two most important landmarks of modern thought and sensibility. For them as well as for Pascal, inner reality and truth were essentially dependent on personal choice and self-understanding. Pascal knew the fear of being alone with oneself, for the true self is absent, except in moments of great tension and faith; Kierkegaard experienced the same anguish when confronted with the nothingness of man without God.

The idea of the nothingness of man by himself and that of the absurdity of his life without God are grounded in experienced reality and in the imagination which apprehends the hopelessness of the human condition if it is deprived of God. This is implicitly Samuel Beckett's world and it is also Kafka's world in which the individual, overwhelmed by guilt and afraid of losing his existence, fully acknowledges all the crimes imputed to him and renounces all aspects of individual self-hood so as to disappear in the mass which surrounds him, showing, in fact, that he longs for nothingness and for the return to the whole.

The notion of absurd which emerges from the works of Edward Lear and Lewis Carroll as well as from those of Ionesco, Adamov and others, is a completely different notion. It involves neither true imagination nor reality; it floats between the two in a world of fancy (splendid fancy, particularly in the case of Lear and Lewis Carroll) where any kind of incoherence, incongruousness and surrealistic associations and contrasts are possible. The workings of the subconscious, as has been proved by the scientific explorations of psychoanalysis, are neither absurd nor meaningless; they have, in the light of reason, a coherence and meaning which is part of the wholeness of the human psyche. But they need to be handled by imagination and not by fantasy, for while the former is connected with reality the latter is not. There is no earthly reason why Ionesco's young woman, in his play entitled *Jacques*, should have only two noses instead of four or five, nor why the corpse in *Amédée* should not stretch to fantastic proportions, nor why men, instead of turning into rhinoceroses should not turn into elephants, hippopotamuses or tortoises. Fantasy can decide what it pleases, since there is no point of reference. Imagination, on the contrary, has always points of reference. Hamlet's ghost, Macbeth's witches, are not fantasies, they are parts of the living experience of the world in which these two characters move; they are real and accepted as such, with as much certainty and truth as the Errenies in Aeschylus's Athens. Fantasy's invention is of a private nature; it has no universal meaning, therefore it can only be accepted by those who wish to do so, as a convention in an intellectual game. It carries no true, affective reality, and intellectual games without any transmutation of reality could hardly be described as poetry.

The Greek world was not absurd; it was on the contrary a closed, and a thoroughly ordered world in which everything that happened was governed by laws and by divinities. The Gods dealt with light, consciousness and being, and Minerva was more important than Juno or Venus. Fate dealt with the incomprehensible, the dark and the mysterious, and curtailed the power of the gods. Transcendence and immanence were one, and life was part of the finality of the Cosmos and was submitted to cosmic and human laws which could not be transgressed without bringing about divine retribution and human justice as is the case with the *Oresteia*. The world of *King Lear* is a world in transition and turmoil, and although men might be, as Gloucester says, "As flies to wanton boys are we to the Gods, they kill us for their sport", there are gods; they may even be the same gods who in Plautus "played games with men as balls", but these gods are indulging their own cruel ways in a world which has its laws. Lear, deeply rooted in his old hierarchical world, cannot understand the individualism and the immanentist values of the new age; yet though his world may be in turmoil, it is not an absurd world. Such a notion would be an insult to the genius of Shakespeare who brings every one of his major, archetypal conflicts, through suffering and death, to a resolution and a reconciliation with the order of nature.

Hamlet is no hero of the absurd. His depth of vision, his sensibility, his unfailing awareness of the naked truth, make it impossible for him to adjust himself to the turpitudes which surround him and to reconcile his religious horror of uncleanliness with the corrupt world in which he has to live. His paradise lost—the world of his father has been destroyed by a "snake" who poured poison in his father's ear and infected his mother— Eve and all women—with a bestial, repellent sensuality. Hamlet is the redeemer whose natural purity makes it difficult for him to overcome his doubts and to accept the burden of his existential tasks. But once he has understood that death is his destiny, he speedily disposes of Rosencrantz and Guildenstern and returns to face his fate, symbolised by Yorick's skull which the grave-diggers present to him in the cemetery to which, in fact, he already belongs. He dies, having performed the traditional duty of the hero, that is to say, after having cleansed the Kingdom by giving up his life and after having prophesied the advent of Fortinbras to the Throne. He believes that once he has performed the sacrificial and ritualistic task which his unique vision imposed upon him, the time has come for Fortinbras, the man of action, to rule over his redeemed Kingdom. In a similar way, Lear's suffering and mind-wrenching sorrows have not been in vain; they have taught him the true plight of the human condition, they have unsealed his eyes to the true meaning of love. In the world of apparent immanence in which he lived, Cordelia's death touches him as an act of grace which prefigures supernal reconciliation and which transfigures his death with an aura of joy which shows that transcendence, though in abeyance, had not disappeared, and that though the ways of Providence may be unfathomable, neither a leaf nor a sparrow ever falls without playing its part in a cosmos in which man's acceptance of the experiences which come to him is the only way to wisdom and peace. "... Men must endure their going hence, even as their coming hither: Ripeness is all. . . ."

The notion of the partial absurdity of life within certain conditions can neither be applied retroactively to ages which accepted the notion of a cosmic order and that of human ignorance and finitude, nor generalised. The absurdist who confines absurdity to life's coherence and purpose is an absurdist in the way Montaigne and Valéry were sceptics, that is to say, sceptics who wrote books so that other people could read about their scepticism which, if it had been shared by their prospective readers, would of course have made of them non-readers. Therefore, this type of absurdism is only an attitude of mind, a fear, a way of looking at life but not an absolute. Nietzsche himself, who is more than anybody else responsible for the spread of the notion of nihilism and absurdity, summed up this point in these words: "That I have basically been a nihilist is something that I have only recently come to admit. The energy, the radicalism with which I forged ahead as a nihilist deceived me with respect to this basic fact. When one pushes on towards a goal it seems impossible that aimlessness itself should be the basis of our faith." One could not find a more cogent denial of the notion of total absurdity and nihilism, by the master who is all too aware that the passion with which he preached his creed is a form of idealism which belies his very preaching. "Aimlessness itself" is not possible in existence, so that absurdity and nihilism are only passing states, parts of historical moments which can partially affect existence, but cannot involve the whole of it.

The worship of science tends to replace man's spiritual centre by a set of anthropocentric notions which can no more hold together the various aspects of human life than dust can hold together the stones of a house. Yet scientific enquiries and discoveries of the law of nature, logical analyses of human actions and psychological studies of the human psyche could never rationally explain man's search for God. This type of dogmatic rationalism can only satisfy those who believe in it, and since its truth cannot be demonstrated, it can only be tested, like the belief which it seeks to dethrone, upon the pulse of human experience. By this test it will be found that the man who believes is at least as rational as the man who professes not to, for he does not outrage reason by turning its limitations into hollow dogmatic assertions. This type of reason is what Whitehead described as one-eyed reason and instead of being man's true essence and light, it is man's blinkers aimed at concentrating his gaze on empiricism and materialism. To be rational means to accept the limitations of reason and not try to measure the infinite with the inch tape of the finite. It means that one can be both sceptical and tolerant about the beliefs which reason cannot disprove. It does not, certainly, mean replacing the religious fanaticism which reason rightly opposed and destroyed, by rational fanaticism, something which is an obvious contradiction in terms.

The question whether or not life is worth living cannot be disposed of by logical analyses and grammatical investigations. The formulation of this question might be aired a good deal by such examinations. Its content cannot be exhausted by such means; it will always retain an impenetrable core which cannot be rationalised; it can only be lived or not lived. These alternatives are the only two types of existential judgements which can settle this very individual question, and in either case, the basic motives remain a matter of conjecture and not of demonstrations. The sleight of hand consisting in replacing the mysterious energy which informs life and which the Christians ascribe to God, by any kind of terminology one may like, neither solves the problem nor dispels men's anxiety and dread. Anxiety affects both religious and non-religious people, for, contrary to Marxists and other atheists who believe that religion is a kind of drug which enables those who have faith to live in a fool's paradise, the true Christian who searches for God or whom God has found, can never think that such a state is final and that it will enable him to remain with his Maker. The true believer lives, like Claudel's Prouhèze, with a hook in his gills and he cannot, he would not, presume to know whether God will, in the end, fish him out. If living on the razor-edge between ineffable bliss and such utterly unfathomable sorrow is not truly more tragic than any notion of absurd, then nothing else is.

The critics of Christianity always clamp their rational dogmatism on the very nature of true Christian faith and they assert that anyone who has it, who dies for it or within it, cannot suffer a tragic death. This is a complete misunderstanding, by professed atheists, of the true nature of faith as witnessed by the examples quoted above. Faith is not reconcilable with certainty, and the odds which involve eternity for those who believe in it, are certainly more tragic than those who confine life to being a flicker which surges from the dust of nothingness and purely and simply returns to it. Where is the tragedy since there is nothing left to endure it? On the brevity or on the meaninglessness of life? That cannot be tragic since only man's reason deems that it is so; he could therefore very well adjust himself to it and take it as it is, or rather as he thinks it is. The tragic element implies a cotangency of circles which atheism does not posit. It implies a human world and a cosmic world of which man is a part; it implies finite and infinite, and it is the interplay of these two circles which makes the tragic. God is not there to solve problems, He is there to make them, and if only the atheists could understand this point, they would cease wrapping themselves up in cloaks of noble stoicism and courage, while they look upon their religious-minded fellow beings as half-drugged morons led by the hand towards luminous pastures by a host of bearded patriarchs who protect them from every worry and fear. The great ages of tragedy were ages in which transcendence and immanence were still connected; they are so, implicity, in the Shakespearean world, while in Racine they are a blend of Greco-Jansenist notions. Oedipus and Orestes feared the gods and submitted to harsher tests than Job, and when at last they died, they could not be sure that their calvary had a meaning and a finality. All they knew was that their great souls' peregrinations were not finished and that the spirit of their bodily shapes would go on playing a part on earth.

Nietzsche believed what every Greek statue taught us that the beautiful is only negation and absence; Valéry said "the colour of a thing is, amongst other colours, that which it repels and can't assimilate". From the Greeks, right up to the end of the "Age of reason", knowledge has been something objective, except of course the "cogito" of Descartes. Rationality, although it never embraced the whole of life, embraced the full range of knowledge which was, on the whole, with the exception of Pascal's "raisons du cœur", intellectual knowledge. By the end of the eighteenth century, the limitations of reason were becoming more and more apparent, and imagination, which had been condemned and distrusted by Plato, as well as by Hobbes, Pascal, Descartes and Locke, was asserting its pre-eminence as the only valid source of a type of knowledge which eludes the rational and which is creative knowledge. It began to be more and more recognised, in spite of the rising tide of positivism, that the core of mystery which is the being of the phenomenal world and which Kant called the thing-in-itself, could only be hinted at or suggested so as to be intuited through imagination, but not rationally described.

English romanticism marks the breakaway from conceptualism which never developed in England the same deep roots as it did in France, and asserts the pre-eminence of imagination in a poetry full of suggestiveness and imprint with the sense of the numinous and of the immanent spirituality which informs the universe. In France, with the striking exception of Delacroix and with some minor exceptions like Sainte-Beuve, Watteau's wistfulness and shudder at the fleetingness of time has turned into the melancholy, tearful introspectiveness of Rousseau, Chateaubriand and Lamartine and into the conceptualisation of subjectivity, exoticism and medievalism, which lasted well into the second half of the nineteenth century. By then, the Spinozan beliefs in the wholeness of the Cosmos, to which was added the Schopenhauerian belief in the inter-dependence of the senses began to dominate the arts. Poetry became above all "Voyance", suggestiveness, discovery of mysterious meanings, and a symbolic equivalence of the creator's experience. Such an experience, which was both sub-jective and cognitive, could, once it was embodied in the objectivity of the work of art, be fully or partially apprehended in its reality through intuition which sought to re-create it. Knowledge became thus an act of consciousness or rather an act of self-consciousness, for knowing really meant knowing oneself in the act of knowing. This trend was to continue and to be steadily increased by the progress of psychology until, with Valéry, Proust, Joyce and other post-symbolists and cubists, artistic knowledge was essentially self-knowledge and the search for the absolute which fascinated both Mallarmé and Valéry. There was of course, side by side with that, the mid-century wave of positivism which appealed to the middle class, fully engrossed in the rising materialism of the industrial revolution and which was tossed about between facile optimism, superficial rationalism, sentimentality and religious apathy. The results of this attitude were naturalism, melo-drama, vague aestheticism, didacticism and escapism. In con-tradistinction to these aspects of art favoured by the middle class, we have art for art's sake and the artist's total disgust for an insensitive society which drove him to exile, or under-ground where he used art as a code for initiates.

By the end of the nineteenth century, positivism and materialism were in full retreat, and the artists boldly emerged from their exile and their clandestinity to continue their absorbing self-explorations in a language which was less esoteric, though certainly not meant for mass communication, except in the theatre. Yet, such was, at that time, the interest for poetry and for works of imagination, that even the very difficult works of Jarry and Apollinaire were performed and acclaimed, to say nothing of those of Claudel, while Valéry, Maeterlinck and Rostand achieved world-wide fame. The first world war shattered this blissful climate, and irrationalism, of which war is the most telling example, gained the upper hand with surrealism in the arts. The surrealist experiment was neither long nor conclusive, although it certainly was fruitful as a cleansing, stimulating wind which fostered new growths. Post-symbolist subjectivism and allusiveness reasserted themselves with Valéry, Eliot, Supervielle, Pierre-Jean Jouve, Eluard and Emmanuel, while Yeats, freed from his early romantic mistiness, was applying his superb imagination to the transcendence of the real and to giving to his personal experiences and those of his nation, the hues of universality. So much for poetry, which, continuing its post-symbolist and imagist impetus with poets like Pound, Eliot, Wallace Stevens, Hart-Crane, Robert Lowell, Muir, and the whole admirable group of English poets ranging from Auden and Dylan Thomas to Ted Hughes, has not, in spite of the age of anxiety, entirely retreated from the world and from the object and still uses them as starting points for imaginative creations.

Art, on the contrary, has turned away from the object, and, aspiring like symbolist poetry to the condition of music, it began by replacing the object with a complex of forms and relationships representing the experience called forth by the object. The next step was to eliminate the object entirely. As anti-naturalism was by then in the ascendancy in all the arts, painting took the same direction. The object was a hindrance to the artistic imagination whose aim became not to reproduce, but to give an equivalence of remembered sensations, and just as in music, the notes are, or at least, ought to be, nothing but themselves, in painting, form is all, in the same way as in poetry the poem is not what it says, but what it is. Since reality can no longer be apprehended as a whole, as was the case when man still believed in the supremacy and universalism of reason, the artist is now convinced that the attempt to impose unity upon reality can only be superficial conceptualism without any relation to truth which, in the wake of Kant, Kierkegaard and Nietzsche, has become more and more subjective and existential. The only reality which man can attempt truly to know is the experienced reality of his own consciousness. Artistic creation is therefore the objectification of the consciousness of the artist who is both at the same time the priest and the sacrificial victim in whom the truth rests. Art is the symbolic equivalence of an individual self-consciousness apprehending itself in the act of being self-conscious. It is the snake biting its tail, locked in a luminous circle which radiates truth. This kind of truth, unprocessed by a conceptualised and artificially imposed order, is necessarily of a composite nature, as if it were made of a constellation of phosphorescent points which together form a picture, but which convey no meaning in separation. The most significant modern poetry has been of this nature; so is modern painting, particularly in its cubist phase, and so is music. It sounds synthetic, it is simply an image of fragmented reality.

The artist is intent upon self-knowledge, for it is only by knowing himself that he can be a useful examplar to his fellow-beings. By exteriorising his subconscious—the domain of darkness—he exteriorises also that of his fellow-beings and that of his age, and by so doing he helps his age to become conscious of itself and to hasten the transformations and changes upon which the life-force is intent. Great art, great actions and great men derive their strength from the subconscious, archetypal forces which they express. Modern art expresses a great deal of the anxiety, despair, introspectiveness and self-destructive urge of our age obsessed by violence and by the terror of the forces which it has unleashed and which, for the moment, it has not mastered. Yet, this art is in itself a token of man's faith in the future and a sign that, irrespective of his fears, he pursues his search for his true spirit.

CHAPTER TWO

TRAGEDY AND NATURALISTIC DRAMA

DRAMA, like all the arts, oscillates between imitation or reproduction of reality and its transmutation by imagination into a symbolic object. Imitation or reproduction of the appearance of reality implies, above all, craftsmanship. Transmutation implies an essential correspondence between the inner structure of the objects or experiences, bases of art, and the inner structure or essence of the subject who records such a correspondence in words, musical notations, colours or shapes, so as to produce a symbolic equivalence of the experience of knowing himself and the truth he was searching for, in moments of true being. True being is therefore never the outcome of a solipsistic act, but always a moment of union, whether it is union with the whole, as in mysticism, or union of a subject with an object or with the intent or purpose of his consciousness. This act is an intuitive act and a revelation of a hitherto unknown truth, a kind of transference of colours on an apparently neutral surface which possessed, in fact, both the necessary chemical virtualities to receive these colours and the skeletal patterns to which these colours could give shape and existence. Once this picture has imprinted itself upon the imagination, the mind, partly as a vast computer, automatically begins to decompose and to classify its component parts, and partly as the conscious instrument of the intentionality of the artist, continues, through deduction and induction, to explore this revelation of intuition until the greater part or even the whole of it becomes an object of cognition.

Painting and sculpture require more craftsmanship than poetry and music and have therefore always carried more imitations and reproductions of reality than either, although they have produced, of course, as great imaginative trans-mutations. The genius of Michelangelo and Da Vinci is at least equal to, if not more wide ranging than, that of Dante or Shakespeare. In modern times, painting and sculpture having moved further and further away from reproductions or representations of natural objects, towards imaginative renderings of experiences, craftsmanship has tended to be reduced to a minimum. Music, in its most inspired aspects, has also moved in the same direction. The experimental novel, particularly in France, also tends towards an objectified world of things which had been fully explored by Cézanne and which had been, probably unintentionally, anticipated by Flaubert in *Salammbô*, and of course intentionally by the imagist poets. Flaubert had aimed at creating an atmosphere by an accumulation of carefully and minutely described de-tails which form a vivid pictorial background to the plot. The banqueting scene of the beginning is two or three galleries of the British Museum compressed into a few pages; the moon rising over Carthage, the ritualistic scene between Salammbô and the serpent, the death of Mathô, are scenes worthy of the brushwork of a great painter. The characters themselves look as if they were part of a painting, and they have therefore a certain mechanical rigidity or a kind of hieratic stance which blends them with the background which Flaubert has so lovingly described in order to infuse life into them. Flaubert could not feel himself into Salammbô in the way he felt him-self into Madame Bovary, or Shakespeare had felt himself in Hamlet, and so in a Cézannesque fashion, he concentrated on the thingness of the objects surrounding the characters. His imagination being autobiographical and visual, Salammbô's and Mathô's figures do not fully emerge with a life of their own from the glittering, exotic atmosphere with which he has masterly surrounded them. The *nouvelle vague* novelists practise a form of phenomenalism which excludes or tries to keep at bay the human and to concentrate on the thingness of things, and not on plot and character. It must be said that this movement, in spite of the clamour of *avant-garde* critics, is merely a straw in the wind compared with the traditional humanity-laden novels of Faulkner, Hemingway, Steinbeck, Graham Greene, Pasternak, Sartre, Mauriac, Moravia, Angus Wilson, Iris Murdoch and other novelists with well-deserved reputations.

Drama is the most impure and the most social of the arts. Its subject is not man alone, whether in a Promethean stance of metaphysical rebellion and defiance or singing of his sorrows and woes in solitary meditation; it is man in relationship to other human beings or to perennial forces which come into play through human beings. The forces which are at work in the tragedies of Aeschylus and Sophocles are more teleological than psychological, and their impact and range is as much suggested by the choral recitatives as by the actions and thoughts of the protagonists of the drama; yet, although many of the human beings involved in these tragedies are archetypal and far beyond the mould of ordinary psychology in the sense that they are both the playthings of the gods and the embodiments of superhuman forces, they are nevertheless recognisably human. Clytemnestra is both the recipient of the Atrides' curse and a royal woman, capable of lust, envy, jealousy and of regal anger. Electra does not lack human reality either, and her hatred of her mother could, up to a point, be rationalised and turned to account by a modern psychologist. The outraged majesty and unspeakable sorrows of Oedipus find harrowing echoes in the human heart, whether Greek or modern. Drama is fundamentally an imitation of action in order to convey to an audience or to a reader, the emotions and thoughts of people involved in conflict or in interacting one upon the other, whether the causes are more or less supernatural, or purely human. The more the causes and conflict tends towards the supernatural or towards the archetypal, the more the dramatic action takes on the appearance of a ritual. Greek drama was essentially ritualistic. The plight of Lear or Hamlet is on such a scale that it ranges from the profoundly human desperation which grips these two hypersensitive, sorely tried human beings, to the heroic and mythical stature of heroes standing at the fountain-head of certain aspects of human sensibility which they so perfectly sum up and crystallise that, since their emergence into imaginative creations, men have not been able to think of or to attempt to explore the realm of human sensibility which they embody, without descrying or summoning their presence.

Painting and sculpture may tend towards abstraction or mental transmutations of experience, and poetry may try in vain to emulate the purity of music, but drama is unavoidably grounded in human reality and actions which are, by definition, impure. There are of course moments of pure poetry in Shakespearean drama, and such moments are even more numerous and sustained in Greek drama with the pure lyricism of the chorus; but drama is meant to be enacted and not recited, and as such, it requires an audience which must be given the possibility of apprehending the meaning and import of actions through action. Plays can, of course, be enjoyed as much, and in certain cases more, in the solitude of the study; yet, only those who have imagination can do their own staging and acting. Most people need to see a play acted in order to be able to come to grips with it. All playwrights are aware of the need for an audience and of the fact that a play is only finished once it has been fused into a dramatic experience by the interaction of actors and audience. W. B. Yeats wanted "an unpopular theatre, an audience like a secret society ... and mysterious art doing its work by suggesting, not by direct statement, but by complexity of rhythm, colour and gesture". He refused to make the slightest concession to the audience's taste and he had the courage to face up to his isolation from the theatre which he loved. He was perhaps, like Stendhal, prepared to wait a hundred years for his fame; happily he did not have to wait so long. His compatriot Synge was certainly not like that; and above all, the greatest playwright of the modern world, Shakespeare, was not like that either. He could reconcile pure genius, which is revelation of perennial truths, with the contingent world in which he lived and the longings and likings of his audience.

Over-concern with the audience, either in order to amuse it so as to be successful by pandering to its tastes, or in order to expound one's own political or religious point of view, can testify to craftsmanship, journalistic acumen, flair for what is wanted and pliancy and skill to supply it, but it cannot lay serious claims to art. This kind of writing has of course a place in the entertainment world, neither to be despised nor to be neglected and can be both exciting and financially rewarding, but its impact is as fleeting as that of a football match or a circus performance and it could hardly be described as an enriching experience. It no doubt entertains, and so of course does true art, but there is a world of difference between the entertainment derived from watching a play by Chekov, Beckett or Brecht, and that derived from watching a factory-made television play or a slick reproduction of a dramatic formula which has proved its appeal to the broad public. The theatre lends itself all too easily to the imitation of a formula which has been found successful. Beckett's tramps, Brecht's prostitutes and Jimmy Porterism have already had quite a progeny and are the stock-in-trade of skilful craftsmen. Craftsmanship, of course, is not without importance, and it is not to be despised, for there is no possible great art without it. Shaw and many who came after him rightly scoffed at Scribe's dramaturgy which, when it was used without much substance, was pure and simple mechanicalness, hollow and boring; but when such watertight dramatic constructions were also vehicles for the actions and interactions of profound studies in characterisation, as it the case with Ibsen, the result is one of the highest achievements in world drama.

Now, there is, in certain spheres of drama, a similar disregard for construction and for organicity, and a reliance on mood and social or affective excitement as media for producing drama. The result is arbitrarily determined slices of life or successions of tableaux, not uninteresting in certain cases, but without beginning or end, and bearing little resemblance to a dramatic action which ought to be something organic with a beginning, an interplay of human emotions and actions, and an end which is a form of resolution of the conflict or interplay of human relationships. These plays are only a small proportion of world drama at the moment and they will probably be of very little import; they are a throw-back towards naturalism, the kind of naturalism which, in the literary field, had been fully exploited by Zola and his followers and by Galsworthy, Becque, Antoine and others. This return to naturalism, particularly in England, should not be labelled realism since philosophically it is practically its antithesis. Realism, philosophical realism, implies the existence of a transphenomenal, informing substance of supernatural or noumenal origin; it is the idea of Plato, the essence of Aristotle, the subsistent form of Christian thought or the "noumenon" of Kant. Therefore he who believes in realism will repudiate all attempts at confining reality to its appearance, and if he is an artist, he will seek to discover through his art, this informing reality through imagination and through syntheses of appearances and not through photographic reproductions of appearances. Naturalism denies the existence of any active informing substance and reduces the world to material elements, therefore it is an exact description of material elements. It is not difficult to see that the attempts to exactly reproduce a given aspect of reality is merely a distortion and a falsification of the true reality which can only be apprehended through imagination extracting the essential elements of any given object or experience and embodying them into an imaginative entity or symbol.

Art, though it is unavoidably relative, must nevertheless convey an impression of totality of being and of an all-embracing aspect of life more real than life itself, which can never be apprehended as a whole but always sequentially. The aim of art is totality of experience, and all its component elements must be congruent and an integral part of the whole. In drama all the elements must be congruent to the action, or if there is no action, to the central situation which is the kernel of the dramatic interest. "A drama", said Gorki, "must be bound by its action, strictly and throughout; only with this condition can it serve to arouse contemporary emotions." If, as is the case with tragedy or with static plays of situations, like *Waiting for Godot*, there is strictly speaking no dramatic suspense, no anxiety as to the denouement which is either known or is not crucial to the mechanism of the play, there must nevertheless be an absolute congruence of all the elements, whatever they are, to the movement or central theme of the drama.

The exact relationship between social factors and artistic creation is something impossible to ascertain with accuracy and the attempt to do so generally ends in the dilemma of the hen and the egg. Society can either encourage or frustrate genius, particularly in the case of drama which is pre-eminently a social art. Nothing can stifle genius, although limitations, whatever their origin, can restrain and compress it; yet, whether it painfully soars, carrying with it the remains of its broken shackles or rises to greater heights through the compressions which surround it, genius consists as much in transcending the difficulties which lie in its path as in finding the themes and situations through which it can express its essence. The classical age imposed upon tragedy shackles which genius transcended but which burdened talent and contributed to the disappearance of tragedy, which only re-emerged with the Romantics. Between these two periods lie the full ascendancy of rationalism, prose, the middle class, the emergence of bourgeois drama, and above all, the emergence of the novel which from the latter half of the nineteenth century onwards has tended more and more to be the dominant form of literature. While before, playwrights and poets mostly wrote for kings and for the élite which lived at court, now with the shift of social gravity towards the middle class, the writer could no longer neglect this fast expanding market.

The roots of the middle class were necessarily shallow; its tastes were uncertain and did not, on the whole, tend towards nobility, sacrifice and ritualistic death. That was normal for the nobility schooled in the ritual of chivalry and trained to see in war and death the supreme human test. The middle class, like all middle classes, wanted to live comfortably, with just enough sentiment and romance to add spice to life, but certainly not to cause deep disturbances. What it wanted from the arts was an illusion of the world of which it dreamt, and a form of art easy to grasp, flavoured with just enough vague sentimental pathos to cause a thrill, and of course with a happy ending. This fashion still prevails in our time. It certainly did not want tragedy; it had enough with its own petty or individual sorrows; it preferred to have its senses titillated by the ups and downs of melodrama. The playwrights who wrote for the middle class could not hope to appeal to the élite, and as the middle class offered a much wider market, the prerequisites for melodrama and large-scale entertainments certainly out-balanced the prerequisites for tragedy and public communion in a form of dramatic ritual. The answer was the *comédie larmoyante.*

The great poets of the Romantic age who were all very anxious to write for the stage, did not have a sympathetic audience. Beside that, one must acknowledge the important fact that the lyric mode is anything but the same as the dramatic mode. A poet, as has been made clear by Tennyson or Browning, may write brilliant dramatic monologues, and yet not be capable of making two, three or four characters speak in turn and above all, each with his own individual voice; it is of course not much good if they all speak with their maker's voice. The lyrical, recitative tone which perfectly suits one single, though modulated voice, does not easily pass from one mood to another. The lyric imagination can probe deeply and above all can afford to become fully self-engrossed in the fluctuations of its own consciousness. The dramatic imagination cannot allow itself to be so completely caught up in one single type of emotion or cogitation; it cannot plunge down and lengthily dwell in the depths; it must remain continuously on the wings, swiftly moving from one point to another, keeping them all illumined and in fact directing a well-orchestrated dance of fires and not dealing with one single bonfire. The great Romantic writers, particularly the English and the French, were essentially lyrical poets, and their attempts at drama show clearly enough the predominance of this trait. In spite of Keats's wonderful assertion that the poet ought to be endowed with the "negative capability" of being anything, they were above all themselves. Their characters, from Hernani and Prometheus to Faust, reflect all too clearly their own personalities, and they are still too obviously connected with them in a way in which Shakespeare's or Racine's characters are not connected with their creators. They all admired Shakespeare, raved about him and some, like Victor Hugo, translated him, but they all tried to draw him to themselves and not to take him for what he was. While Shakespeare treated history with the utmost poetic licence, they, belonging to an age when history was very much debated and considered important, treated history with great reverence. Shakespeare for them was in fact, part of history, like Gothicism and Medievalism, and what captured their historical imaginations were the violent contrasts of his characters and their daemonic passions from which they were dissociated by intervening centuries of rationalism. They sought to revive these passions, and the romantic hues through which they gazed at Hamlet were transferred upon Werther and Hernani, while Cordelia's were transferred upon Marguerite and Doña Sol. The one who showed that he had grasped some aspects of the atmosphere of Shakespeare's plays is Schiller who is also the best dramatist of the Romantic age. Goethe, once he had regained, at some cost, his Appollonian calm, could not reconcile the tragic outlook with his love of science and his belief in perfectibility. The Romantics certainly believed in the virtues of suffering, but they could no longer piece together the world which rationalism had destroyed, and without such a unified world, the kind of poetic drama of which they were dreaming could not live. They lived in a fragmented world, haunted, not by ghosts and visitations from above, but by science and scientific optimism which were totally alien to tragedy. As the poets could not ignore science, some of them carried on strange love-hate associations with it. Besides that, by the second half of the nineteenth century, the poets were seriously challenged by novelists of outstanding genius whose popular support and readership left poetry behind, in spite of the great success of Tennyson; so, some of the plays of the great Romantic poets were not even performed in their lifetimes.

Ibsen, Chekov and Strindberg appeared just in time to prevent tragedy from sinking to the level of a purely academic subject. Ibsen, who is one of the giants among world dramatists, realised that no great art is possible without an organic order which, if it is not inherited, has to be created on its own terms. Every artist of importance has to inherit or to create his own universe in which the growth of his art is an organic development which is held together in a congruence of movement.

Shakespeare and Racine inherited theirs. Ibsen, Maeterlinck and Chekov had to make their own. Cézanne did the same; Rilke made his with his special angels, Kafka with his castles and strange cities, Joyce with his Odyssean journey, Lawrence with his dark gods and Picasso with his tauromachy; Yeats constructed his with his lunar phases and his complex mixture of Platonic symbolism, Irish legends and Eastern philosophy. Claudel and Eliot found theirs in Christian religion, and, from the end of the nineteenth century to our times, many dramatists have sought to make or to strengthen the poetic atmosphere of their plays by fusing modern sensibility with Greek myths. Ibsen created his own mythology, symbolism and his own powerful forces which drive his characters towards the type of unbearable, luminous self-knowledge which is the very essence of tragedy. Once any dramatic character has reached such a knowledge, he can only take poison, like Phèdre, or jump from a bridge like Rebecca, or from a tower like Solness. Ibsen achieved the unique *tour de force* of clothing his characters in a type of reality which is both clearly recognisable and, at the same time, tinged with supernatural and pertaining to all men at all times. He alone in his age could reconcile, at their highest level, the perfect blend of realism with poetic imagination. Brand starts from the earth and rises to the clouds, and Hedda Gabler, firmly planted on the earth, blazes with a consuming flame which leaves behind it the ashes of poetry. Chekov and Strindberg, endowed with lesser gifts, performed upon reality the same transmutations as Ibsen, and some of their plays reached a tragic level. In our time, this level has sometimes been reached by W. B. Yeats, Synge, Claudel, O'Neill, Eliot, Giraudoux and Montherlant.

This is not a random list, although it certainly can be argued about, and no doubt altered; the fact that Brecht's name is not included in it makes it clear that it is not a list of the best playwrights of our time, for any such list would have to include his name, even if it contained only two or three others. Besides that, there is the name of Sean O'Casey who is one of the leading modern playwrights and there are those of Sartre, Tennessee Williams, Miller and Anouilh, who are practically as important, and who have not been included among the list of authors of tragedy. Why tragedy? Because, bearing in mind the modifications which tragedy has undergone throughout the ages from Aeschylus to Ibsen, it still remains the highest form of drama. A second-rate or a mediocre tragedy is not, of course, worth a good comedy, but all in all, it seems possible to push this kind or argument to its extreme and to say that a tragic masterpiece like *Lear* offers a more profound and richer aesthetic experience than any other masterpiece of a different nature like, for instance, *The Misanthrope*, or a straightforward comedy. One is perfectly aware that there are differences of temperament and that there are many people who will derive greater satisfaction from the latter type of play than from the former, but all in all, it seems to me possible to say that the contemplation of the terror and pity which flow from Lear's and Cordelia's fate, the heart-rending sorrow which their unavoidable collision has unleashed and the wisdom which finally emanates from Lear's blindness, have a far more moving and penetrating effect than the pathos derived from truth-loving Alceste trapped in a world of lies and deceit and in love with a coquette. One feels deeply affected by the web of human contradictions and paradoxes which surround Alceste's life, but one does not come out of this play as one comes out of *Lear*, with the feeling that one has journeyed through centuries and with one's emotions and thoughts (I add thoughts for the Brechtians) transmuted and fused into an experience which, from then on, will always be part of the glass of conscience through which we shall look at reality.

The problem of tragedy is therefore not an academic problem but on the contrary something of vital importance to the theatre. Life without a sense of tragedy is a medley of futilities and facile optimism in which man needs neither the noble curiosity which leads him to shape his environment and so to discover the laws of the universe, nor the sense of tragic grandeur which enables him constantly to risk the gamble of his own individual existence against the nothingness which is the alternative to being. Whatever the arts one is dealing with, the sense of tragedy and noble conflict and the self-consuming awareness that man can rise like a phoenix from the ashes of self-annihilation, from time to eternity, is truly the peak of human achievement. Christ showed the way in his wilful self-oblation, and the most Christian of poets—Dante—shows the turpitude and terrors which surround human life and the nakedness and the scorching fires which the human being, thirsting for the absolute, has to endure before he can approach the realm of outworldly light. The tragic world is neither an absurd world nor a materialistic world. Whether it is enclosed in its religious atmosphere, like the Greek, or is a compound of immanence and transcendence like the Christian, it is a world in which the natural and the supernatural orders are interwoven. It is therefore an organic world in which individual happenings and particular actions connect with the whole. Once these connections are broken, once immanence is separated from transcendence, as it was in the age of rationalism, and as it partly is now in the age of Marxism, the supernatural, the mythical, the legendary and the religious are no longer part of the imaginative reality of the world; they are only part of fancy which uses them as adornments for a conceptualised world.

Ibsen, the greatest landmark in world drama since Racine, had to create his own universe before he could successfully approach the problems of tragedy. Chekov's theatre, infinitely subtle, infinitely complex, in which passion smoulders slowly and people seem to die out of utter boredom and lack of will to live, is also a world of its own. In it, realism is transmuted, made translucent, so as to show its own true reality; it is a kind of pure phenomenalism; reality is all, and reality is not a deception or a mask for something else; reality is itself boring, deceitful and without any hope of final resolution or expression which could transform its nature. With Chekov, there is no Ibsenian progression from ignorance to self-knowledge which calls for death, and no dramatic suspense in a world of elemental passions and poignant suffering. Life is not black and white; it is grey, criss-crossed with wild outbursts of joys and sorrows and continuously smouldering tensions which cannot reach final, liberating explosions and resolutions, as in traditional tragedy. Yet the tension is unbearable and the characters are tragically crushed by the merciless greyness which surrounds them, while they remain locked in their own respective worlds, from which they talk and struggle without being able to join the others. Our modern theorists of the impossibility of communication between men have invented nothing in this domain. Chekov proceeds impressionistically and cumulatively, not in order to produce a complete picture as in a novel, but in order to produce a congruence of movement. He uses details like notes in a musical composition and always in order to rise from the particular to the general, from reality to imagination. He deals with facts and with the middle class, but he either transmutes or intersperses facts with imaginative flights; he deals with characters who are not part of society's élite, but they are varied, vocal, intelligent and capable of insight and poetic vision. The facts which he uses are an integral part of the play's movement, and the greyness of life which some of his plays depict is not represented by inarticulate, down-trodden, subhuman characters who can only mumble platitudes, clichés and political slogans. He carefully shuns the mimetic fallacy, knowing all too well that dullness, boredom, greyness are not conveyed by dull, boring, incoherent plays. He imposes form on these elements and it is the subtle form of a highly complex, poetic imagination. Chekov was a story-teller but he does not use his facts as a story-teller. The time concentration of the dramatic action does not permit that; the passions, thoughts and behaviour of the characters involved are reduced to their dominant aspects, and each detail is part of the dramatic necessity.

Contemporary naturalism, sometimes wrongly described as realism, is of a very different type. First of all, it often carries with it a great deal of didacticism and socal and ethical proselytism, and in some cases it is for its authors what painting professedly was for Courbet—a means of fighting social battles. Besides that, it is above all embodied in a type of drama which is very close to the novel, the dramatised novel, and it is in many cases the work of writers who are primarily novelists, or who, if they write plays, apply to playwriting the techniques of the novel.

Although the difference between drama and the novel are well known, they are nevertheless the cause of a good deal of misinterpretation between what is dramatic and what is not dramatic, and between a dramatised story or a slice of a novel, and dramatic characters locked in conflict. The crucial difference between the two genres is above all that between analytical and synthetic art. The novel analyses, explains and describes characters and the background to which they belong, in their totality; drama is only concerned with the qualities of the characters which sharpen the conflict and prepare the final explosion and resolution of the play or the finale of the symphony, as is the case with Chekov. The aims and differences between these two genres have been sufficiently rehearsed to be fully known by now, yet at this moment when the greater number of films and television plays and a good few stage dramas are not really drama but dramatised novels, novelettes or short stories, they can hardly be overstressed. Even although there are novelists like Ivy Compton Burnett who endeavour to convey the actions, feelings and thoughts of their characters through dialogue, the general way of conveying these elements is through narrative interspersed in varying degrees with dialogue.

The novel, whatever its scope, concerns itself with characters seen in their totality, fully integrated into more or less powerful social forces which find expression in them, and which exteriorise the process of growth or disintegration of a whole social pattern. Drama, even if it deals with the fluctuations of social forces as is the case with Ibsen, Strindberg and Chekov, is not truly concerned with the progress of such a movement, but only with its incidental impact and outcome through the characters; for drama is always a crisis, and a crisis cannot last for long. The minute descriptions of details,

the reflective moments, the lyrical outbursts of passions and emotions, all hamper its dynamism, its overall congruence of movement towards an end. Whatever is not congruent to this movement is extraneous to it, and therefore detracts from its excellence. Movement, whatever causes it, and conflict, whatever its component elements, are universals which transcend the limitations of historical time and social factors. The forces which underlie the movement of Greek drama are no longer objects of reverence and belief, yet beyond the names of these forces which are quite different now, the movement which carries these heroes to destruction is still as impressive and as meaningful for modern scientific mankind as it was in the days of Plato. We know all about the Oedipus complex and we have by now discarded the wrath and ploys of interfering gods, but we have not discarded the sense of mystery and the awareness of the plight of man. Today, when there are no gods and when, for many, there is no God, there is therefore, beyond life condemned to end in dust, nothing which could be a consolation or a balm for the sorrow and anxiety of living it. Nothing is nothing—a fearsome notion to face—when as long as senses and mind work, life means on the contrary something real, tangible and on the whole valuable. We no longer believe in witches or in the possibility of carving kingdoms with dagger and sword, though, up to a point, it can still be done with gold; yet the dizziness, the rise and fall of Macbeth caught in the glaring light of the nothingness which creeps upon him, are as moving now as in the Elizabethan age.

The novel aims at depicting a particular reality at a particular time, and at authenticity and completeness of details. Even when characters rise to the level of types, as in the novels of Balzac or Dickens, or to archetypal proportions as in those of Dostoevski, they do so by accumulations and by a deepening of reality and not by a selection of quintessential elements. The conflicting social, historical, religious forces with which drama deals are embodied in individuals who are essentialised so as to tend towards archetypes, and to be fully congruent to an action which aims at communicating an immediate organic, emotional experience to an audience. "Drama", said Pushkin, "was born in a public square." The novel was born in the silence of solitary readings. The former implies a duration which only lives in the present, the latter implies an imaginary voyage which leisurely takes the reader through the world—past or future—that he is reading about, and allows him all the time he wishes to pause and think. In drama, time is short—maximum three hours, and the possibilities of pondering are non-existent, since the play relentlessly moves on; therefore, the characters must be immediately typical and such as to exhibit at once some of their dominant traits. Fidelity to facts and details is, as Shakespeare masterly demonstrated, unimportant; what matters is verisimilitude of feelings and complete congruence to the progression of the conflict. In drama everything must be reduced to human actions and reactions, and social, political or religious elements must either be subsumed in the human element or stand condemned as irrelevant. The dramatic character must contain all and reveal through his actions the world in which he lives; therefore the more individualised and purely subjective he is, the more he tends towards the universal and towards making of his fate and plight something general and valid for all men. Such a transition from the individual to the general is impossible if the character is fettered by social factors and is, up to a point, the prey of injustices which make of him more a pathetic toy than a tragic hero.

The basic fact is that social drama cannot be tragic because the hero in it is a victim of circumstances and incidents which depend upon the society in which he lives and not upon the ineluctable inner compulsions—psychological or religious—which determine his progress towards self-knowledge and death. Religious and psychic forces are certainly part of society and history, but they are not contingent phenomena; they are the forces which inform them and preside over the making of both society and history. Self-knowledge, knowledge of the true import of past, irretrievable deeds, is the true pursuit of the tragic hero who, once he has discovered the unbridgeable distance between his guilt-ridden self and the ideal world which he is aware of, can only try to reach such a world by the destruction of his self, cause of the gap between what he is and what he could or ought to be. Thence his sense of joy and liberation at the approach of death which may reconcile what life has divided and separated.

The tragic hero does not need to be a noble man, a prince or a six-footer, but his actions and his death must have some historical significance, that is to say they must be the direct result of the conflict between the dominant traits or passions which make up his personality and some of the forces of the world in which he lives. Besides that, he must not be tied down to a social, political or religious group, or a circumscribed moment of time which would reduce him to being a pure and simple manifestation of social and historical contingencies, something which pertains to the novel or the epic but not to drama which requires a completely non-fortuitous dramatic necessity. Although there may be, at times, minor incidents which may seem to be fortuitous, there is no room for them in the pattern of tragedy which is such that the hero's character predestines him to conflicts with forces which he cannot master and to which he is destined to succumb. Yet the conflict releases essential historic forces which triumph through the hero's death and therefore enable him to assert his true greatness; thence, the hero's acceptance of death at the end of a conflict which has unfolded according to its own inner laws and necessity, and enables him to find in death the crowning resolution of all oppositions and doubts.

The tragic hero cannot be an abstraction; he must on the contrary be both a particular human being with individual traits and characteristics, and a type, that is to say the embodiment of traits and forces which he shares with a large category of men like him and which therefore make him tend towards the universal. He must be both real, that is to say conform to life as perceived by the senses, and he must have dimensions which pertain to an individual of historical significance or to an imaginative creation or re-creation of such an individual. "To be exact", said Goethe, "nothing is theatrical which does not appear as simultaneously symbolic—an important action indicating one yet more important." The tragic hero must be, like every worth-while artistic creation, a blend of realism and imagination, something which excludes both unadulterated naturalism and fancy. Without any need of being of noble descent, the tragic hero must have a definite nobility of character even if, like Macbeth, he is thoroughly contaminated by evil. He cannot at any moment be sentimental, lost in illusions or pathetically pitiable. He must be unsentimental, un-self-pitying, increasingly aware of his doom, and yet never completely shorn of the noble pride which makes him accept his downfall. He may be, like Miss Julie, the prey of conflicting emotions, circumstances and heredity, but he must retain throughout, as she does, the awareness that while her soulless, social-climbing, class-conscious valet-lover can reconcile himself with any low, despicable deed as long as it leads him to success, her sense of honour does not permit her to do so, for she knows that, come what may, death is the only way of paying for and of annihilating her past errors. Whether the illumination which finally comes to the tragic character compels him to death, or confirms the unbearable futility and pathetic plight of the human situation, as is the case with many Chekovian characters, tragedy must have a kind of ritualistic aspect which involves its protagonists in a public conflict shared and understood by the whole society in which it takes place, and not in a private conflict confined to a social group or to a class of society. Therefore society must offer an image of organic wholeness in which all things, including mythology and symbolism, are connected, so as to give imaginative reality the archetypal depth which it requires, if it is to range beyond historical time and national boundaries and be valid for all men.

Tragedy requires tragic emotions, tragic themes and a society which has the sense of tragedy, something which seems to be singularly lacking at this moment in our fragmented world. Marxism, which is not simply confined to Communism, but embraces also a good deal of socialist thought, is naturally averse to the sense of tragedy. For the believer in Marxism, all will be well in the end, with much greater certainty than for the one who believes in God. The latter is never sure of being in a state of grace, the former rationalises himself into it, and looks upon the ups and downs of real life and the plagues of wars as mere passing phases on the road to the final triumph of the proletariat. Art in Marxist countries can neither be naturalistic nor pessimistic, nor purely idealistic; it can only show society as it should be and those who do not see it that way are traitors to the working-class cause. So, in spite of a form of determinism which is as harsh as Greek necessity, one cannot expect any tragedy from Marxism.

The vogue of the cinema and television has given a new lease of life to naturalism which aims at photographic reproduction of reality. The battle against it had been fought and won in practically every country of Europe. Naturalism had begun a long time ago in the eighteenth century when poetry was at a low ebb and when it began to invade the stage as well as the other arts. Wagner and his notion of total drama are certainly at the root of certain notions of staging which followed. The famous Meningen Company, so intent on naturalism and exactitude of details, started from Bayreuth in 1870. Antoine and Stanislavski took over some of their ideas and followed them; yet Schopenhauer, who by then had been dead for ten years, had already expounded an approach to art which was more or less the symbolist theory which triumphed with Baudelaire, Rimbaud and the symbolist poets and was the basis of the opposition to naturalism. "The artist", he said, "explains and translates the nature of things into simple and comprehensible language. Anyone reading or contemplating a work of art must, with his capabilities, contribute to the discovery of the wisdom contained in art. . . . A work of art can function only through the imagination, therefore a work of art must constantly arouse the imagination, and not just arouse but activate. . . . It therefore follows that the artist's work must not supply everything to our senses, but only enough to direct our imagination onto the right path, leaving the last word to imagination." These words are packed with meaning and significance; they not only contain the whole theory of symbolist poetry with their insistence on the nature of art as the expression of the invisible and the importance of imagination and of the thing unsaid, they also connect German idealism and the romantic faith in imagination with the modern theory of art as creativeness, as expounded by Croce and Collingwood and in fact, by most modern painters and poets, right up to Brecht and his concern for wisdom instead of catharsis and identification.

These words, which express the unbroken continuity of organic life and thought, are both an apologia for imagination and for the importance of the mystery which cannot be conceptualised or reduced to naturalistic reproductions, and, strangely enough, they connect with the words of one of the outstanding apostles of rationalism—Voltaire, who had said: "Le secret d'être ennuyeux c'est de tout dire." Voltaire already knew what some of the great masters, like Constable and Delacroix as well as the symbolists, knew, namely that a work of art which is finished to its last details is on a much lower scale than a work of art which allows the imagination its full possibilities of creativeness. That was of course a well-known truth, and Shakespeare, Da Vinci and Rembrandt did not wait to be told by Mallarmé to add a few shadows to their work. *Hamlet*, the *Madonna of the Rocks*, *The Night Watch* are shadowy enough, and the human imagination is endlessly fed by these creative shadows. Many of Da Vinci's paintings and cartoons are unfinished. Balzac criticised the attempt to depict full military campaigns in order to show what a war is. Tolstoy fell into that very mistake; he took incidents here and there, so much so that when he tried to generalise or to paint wide canvases of Napoleonic strategy, he merely conceptualised his own views and guesses. The lovers of naturalism seem to be the only ones unable to grasp the fundamental truth that photographic reproduction of a necessarily limited slice of phenomenal reality distorts or completely misses the true essence of that reality. The Meningen players and their love of details, Antoine and his extreme naturalism, followed by the Moscow Art Theatre, turned the stage into a museum and acting into a perfect mimicry of everyday life. The plays which this type of theatre produced partook of the same naturalism; the spectator could watch his exact image on the stage; he was soon bored with it. Meyerhold, when he witnessed real tramps on the stage in Gorki's play *Lower Depths,* was as incensed as many Parisians were at Antoine's naturalistic excesses. "How can one call someone an actor when he appears on the stage as in real life?" One does not need to wonder what he would have thought of our modern naturalism on the stage and of our cinematic verism. Chekov was on Meyerhold's side against naturalistic productions, and through a combination of genius and patience, he succeeded in having his plays produced as he intended.

The greatest influence against naturalism was the symbolist theatre, and Maeterlinck was its leading light. His was a static theatre in which the characters, caught in a modern kind of determinism, had a puppet-like immobility, and sought to convey their deep feelings by the music of silence and plastic movements, and not by words. There obviously was by then a marked revulsion against excessive violence of speech and naturalistic acting. Deep emotions, it was felt, could only be expressed by music as Wagner tried to do, or through silence and plastic gestures. Again there was nothing new in such a point of view, for beyond romantic exuberance and eighteenth-century melodrama, lie the subdued music of Racine's dialogue as in *Berenice,* the brooding asides of the Shakespearian theatre, and the strange wisdom of Savonarola who had fully understood that poignant emotions are not expressed by wild gestures. "Do not think", he said, "that Mary at the death of her Son, cried out, or walked the streets, tearing her hair and acting like a mad woman. She came to her Son with meekness and great humility." This is at the other extreme of Victor Hugo's drama, and the symbolists went beyond Wagner's attempts to express emotions with music and equated, as Mallarmé, Valéry, Yeats and others suggested, drama with its origin which was the dance. The notion of drama as dance with masks as in the ancient past, or in the Noh plays, seems to have combined with the *Commedia dell'arte* traditions of jugglers, mimicry and improvisation to produce in France a remarkable revival of mimicry with

Marcel Marceau, Decroux and J-L. Barrault. This tradition is the antithesis of naturalism and "method" acting; the action is as openly fictitious as Brecht could wish it. Stage changes and promptings are carried out by the attendants who go about their business openly as they used to in the past and in the Noh plays, and improvisations take place within definite rules, as is the case with music. Without going over the details of a period of literary history which is well known, one ought nevertheless to note for the purpose at hand that by 1893 the answer to the *théâtre libre* and the Moscow Art Theatre, was *le Théâtre d'Art* founded by Paul Fort, which produced poetic plays, French and foreign, from Maeterlinck to Shelley, Shakespeare, Marlowe, Claudel, Hofmannsthal and others; this was followed by the *Théâtre de l'Œuvre* with Jacques Copeau and his successors. Even *Ubu Roi* which, according to Copeau, was *pur théâtre*, synthetic and creating on the margin of reality a reality based on symbols, was produced in 1896. Apollinaire's surrealist play *les Mamelles de Tirésias* followed. The battle, as far as France was concerned, was won. In Russia, Meyerhold tried in vain to deviate from Stanislavski's method, towards abstraction and stylisation of production.

In Germany the influence of Adolphe Appia, much admired by Copeau, restored his place to the actor and developed Wagnerian plastic décors through the skilful use of lighting effects. Gordon Craig developed still further these Wagnerian notions of total drama which were upheld later by Claudel and Jean-Louis Barrault. Max Reinhardt's love of baroque gave these Wagnerian notions his own imprint which satisfied the taste of the rich bourgeois of his day. Antonin Arthaud, whose name cannot be ignored, seemed to put the final touch to the notion of total drama as a means to express what cannot be put into words. "Words," he said, "do not mean everything; by their nature and defining character fixed once and for all, they arrest and paralyse thought instead of permitting and fostering its development." He was against words on the rather specious, Wagnerian notion which is at the opposite of Beethoven's, that deep emotions can only be expressed by music or, as Maeterlinck, Jean-Jacques Bernard and others have suggested, by silence. Together with such a notion there goes the Sartian notion that each man is locked in his own solitude and therefore cannot reach the other except as object of his desires and urge for power. The notion that words are fixed, unchanging entities is something which is completely contradicted by the semantics of any language. Words are fluid, slippery, difficult to get hold of. As Eliot puts it:

> ". . . Words strain
> crack and sometimes break, under the burden
> under the tension, slip, slide, perish,
> decay with unprecision, will not stay in place,
> will not stay still. . . ."

Words can, of course, express deep emotions when great poets handle them; even more, the expressiveness of silence can only be prepared by and rise from words. Gestures, facial expressions play their part, but all these are framed by words, provided, of course, that one remembers that great emotions are not expressed by ranting and verbal outpourings but by the utmost control and precision as displayed by the great masters. What is simpler than: "Je ne l'ai point encore embrassé aujourd'hui" of Andromaque, the "Never, never, never, never, never" of Lear, or "Tomorrow and tomorrow and tomorrow" of Macbeth? As we shall see presently, Beckett's suggestive silences in his best plays, are entirely due to his poetic imagination and to his mastery of words.

CHAPTER THREE

DRAMA IN FRANCE

FOR Maeterlinck, inner thoughts and feelings are what matters and real drama takes place within. Of course he was anything but the first to move in this direction; Ibsen had given the lead, and psychology, which was in the ascendancy at that moment, stressed the importance of inner actions. Maeterlinck looked upon Ibsen's *Master Builder* as a perfect blend of inner and outer dialogue, and Strindberg, who disliked Ibsen, admired Maeterlinck whom he thought a great writer and whom he sought to emulate in his dream plays. In these plays, time does not exist; anything can happen, and imagination can roam about freely and weave any pattern it pleases. The characters are transformed at will to fit the dreamer's subconscious. This is of course, Freudianism without Freud, who did not invent the theories associated with his name. They were already in the air, and in some cases, in circulation, and he co-ordinated and organised them into patterns which bear his name. Strindberg's exacerbated genius pushed both psychology and dreams to the limits of subjectivity and expressionism which flourished at the end of the nineteenth century and at the beginning of the twentieth, and was a form of extreme subjectivism and intuitionism in search of intensity of emotions and expression. It was an attempt to by-pass matter and to grasp the essence of life, and of course, on the stage, it was given full scope with the great developments in the uses of electricity, which dominated staging in the 1920's. The great master was Max Reinhardt who is, with Copeau and Gordon Craig, one of the landmarks of modern stagecraft.

If expressionism is particularly connected with Germany, the French effort to free the theatre from naturalism is

particularly connected with Copeau and the *Vieux Colombier*
and with the use of Greek legends and subjects as means of
separating the audience from reality and of contributing a
climate favourable to the return of poetry to the theatre.
Poetry of the theatre and not poetry in the theatre was
Cocteau's main aim. He mixed dance music and speech, and
his collaboration with Diaghileff and Eric Satie produced
some memorable results. The synthesis of the arts which
Cocteau envisaged, the remarkable gifts which he brought to
such a task, contributed greatly to the anti-naturalist reaction
but did not result in solid achievements which could be
described as landmarks of the theatre. Cocteau's aesthetics,
and his admitedly rich fantasy which is not quite the same as
true creative imagination, rendered such achievements
improbable. Like his friend Diaghileff, he was intent upon
surprise and tried to equate poetry with surprise, with the
unexpected and with the disparate elements which belong
more to the world of fantasy and surrealism than to that of
imagination. His retelling of the story of *Orphée* shows him
at his best, and his retelling of the story of *Oedipus* in *La
Machine Infernale* shows on the contrary that he has no
grasp of tragedy, and merely confirms the lack of sensitivity
which is exemplified by his so-called bird's eye view of the
Antigone of Sophocles and by his trimming up of *Romeo and
Juliet*.

Cocteau is essentially a conjurer, intent upon dazzling the
audience with his skill and tricks, and no doubt he has plenty
of admirers who talk about his work with bated breath and
seek to explain some of his gimmicks and surrealistic fantasies
as being the kind of poetry and music which only the few can
appreciate. Yet Cocteau's encounters with Greek myths have
been anything but successful. Either through incapacity to
understand them, or through wilfulness, he has used them
purely as appearances which stick out of his motley canvases
like heterogeneous pieces of "collage". *La Machine Infernale*
which is his interpretation of the myth of Oedipus is a
prestidigitator's piece of refurbishing which nearly succeeds
in turning a tragic theme into a bedroom farce. The gods are

infernal fiends who play with men as if they were puppets. Oedipus does not need to solve any riddles; the sphinx too impressed by his charm gives him the secret. The soldiers' language and preoccupations are extremely up-to-date; Tiresias becomes Zizi, and the famous brooch, which, in the end, pierces Oedipus' eyes, has been so much talked about that it practically carries out the deed by itself. Oedipus has already rehearsed his coming blindness by thinking that he was blind after looking into Tiresias's eyes. The expressionism is too blatant and the devices and snares to trap the pure hero are so obvious as to be laughable. The conjurer's hand is so clearly evident that the play sinks into melodrama. Cocteau's heroes are all more or less *poètes maudits* marked by defeat from the start and closely related to Tennessee Williams' heroes, except that the latter are either sex-obsessed or sex-starved and that being generally younger than the women with whom they are partnered, they are more or less gigolos. It is obvious that Cocteau is unable to deal with tragic themes, and that although he has had great success, his contribution to drama is likely to be deemed slight.

Anouilh shares with Cocteau the incapacity to grapple with tragic themes but he has a much wider range and he has a dramatic skill unequalled on the contemporary stage. His blend of comedy and seriousness, whimsicality and wry pathos is typically his own, and his remarkably fluent style is a perfect medium for the swift changing moods which it is meant to convey. He moves from naturalism to fantasy with grace and ease, and only O'Casey can so stab comedy with poignancy. With Anouilh, as with Giraudoux and Tennessee Williams, time always degrades and soils. Growing old is a degenerating process, children soon pass from innocence to corruption and pure love cannot live. Happiness is not of this world, and Orpheus, whether born from Cocteau, Anouilh or Tennessee Williams, can only find bliss in death. This is anything but an original attitude; it is nothing else but romantic necrophilia, and Anouilh, who handles this theme with greater success than the other two, has criss-crossed the romantic longing for death with a bitter, social satire and cynicism completely alien to the seriousness of the devotees of Werther and René, although not so remote from Byron's Don Juan.

All Anouilh's heroes are obsessed with purity and with the uncompromising attitude which it entails. Thérèse, Antigone, Joan of Arc, Becket, search for purity and say no to life and to what they call in different ways, *le sale bonheur*. Becket who leads his King to despair through jealousy and unrequited love says no to the King's pleas for reasonableness in the same way as Antigone says *no* to Creon and Joan of Arc to her judges. It is obvious that in each case, these heroes and heroines of negation have been defeated by rational arguments and in fact, say no to reason and logic. "Be logical", says the King to Becket, who replies, "No, it's not necessary, one has only to do absurdly what one has been entrusted with doing to the very end." Absurdly, obviously means without reflection and without reasoning. But the problem is that life not being a series of gratuitous acts, it is rather difficult to set about doing anything absurdly to the very end; although, of course, one may adopt an absurd attitude, which is the case with Anouilh's heroes. In that case the word absurd has a very clear meaning which has no connotations whatever with metaphysical absurdity. It simply means that life degrades and corrupts; therefore, if one wants to remain pure one can only do so by rejecting life. This rejection is absurd in the sense that it cannot be rationally justified; it is a defiance to reason, apparently based on the notion that, reason having failed, life is not worth living. In fact, such an attitude rests upon immaturity and the childish notion that since life cannot be understood, the only way to deal with it is to reject it. Becket does not quite say no because he has failed to understand life; he has not even tried, he is not interested. He was a libertine and a detached hedonist without any principles except that of doing well whatever he did, and when the King appoints him Archbishop, he decides to be the paragon of the function with which he has been entrusted; and so, forsaking the spirit for the letter, he equates the honour of man as well as the honour of God with an absolute no to any aspect of life. He becomes possessed by the game and the game is all. He is what he appears to be. He is a perfect phenomenalist and an example of Pascal's truth contained in the words: "Begin by kneeling down and praying, and faith will perhaps come." Doing whatever one does to the best of one's abilities is an act of faith which can carry with it a sense of truth which may redeem all appearances and inform all actions with true reality. Acting in such conditions ceases being a game and is the real thing, or rather is a means of reaching truth through one's own consciousness and dedication. This means that life itself is only a game or a set of appearances which can only be given reality by what one puts into them. Dramatic action reveals the place where hidden truths lie, and sometimes a character can only reveal his truth by identifying himself with a dramatis persona. Anouilh's plays abound in plays within the play and in masks, impersonations and acting. Playing the game with earnestness is a way of reaching truth and of keeping boredom at bay. The shades of Pirandello are at times hovering very close to Anouilh's theatre.

Jean-Paul Sartre, who cannot claim Anouilh's dramatic skill, has a better mind and a much deeper psychological insight in characters. The only time he made use of Greek myth in *The Flies*, he showed that he had a better and more profound approach to it than Anouilh, Cocteau or Giraudoux. Although he uses the story of Orestes to expound his philosophical creed, his melodramatic play shows coherence and verisimilitude, while there is only pyrotechnics in Cocteau's *La Machine Infernale*. Sartre's views about freedom are certainly questionable, but if one accepts his premise that man makes himself and that whatever he does is his own responsibility, Orestes' defiance of Jupiter and his liberation from guilt are far more moving than Oedipus's destruction by wanton gods. For Sartre, men are not gods' sport; they, on the contrary, rebuff these gods and assume the greatness which pertains to man fully free, and responsible for all his acts and for what he is. Man chooses freely both for himself and for others and he does so without any possible reference to essences or principles which could limit his freedom and

53

lighten the burden of his responsibility; he is in fact constantly forced to struggle with an unavoidable, awe-inspiring freedom which, like a Nessian shirt, he cannot shake off his back, without destroying himself. In the Sartrian world, men, locked in their solitude, afraid of one another, ever engaged in subduing or in avoiding being subdued, tossed about between the aggressiveness and the will to power of subjects and the viscosity of objects, nevertheless say yes to life and do not seek refuge in non-being which for them is *le néant*. On the contrary, they assert themselves or make themselves against nothingness. Sartre wilfully confuses essence—substance of life, and essence—the graph or ashes of a human existence. A man is admittedly the sum of his acts and thoughts and therefore he creates, or one might say, reveals, his own essence which can only be assessed at the end of his existence; but that kind of essence is not the same as the essence or energy which causes him to exist. The notion that man lives in a vacuum, continuously making himself without anything to cling to, is difficult to hold. Man is obviously part of history and of creation, and as such, he is part of a continuum which he influences and which influences him. This continuum exists, has a past which we partly know and a future we partly guess.

This can only be described as absurd if one wishes to play at being all-knowing, like God, or if one wishes to bury one's head in the sand. Sartre professes neither of these attitudes, yet, whenever it suits him, he declares that the world is absurd, although to be met with man's full sense of personal responsibility. How or why, Sartre does not explain and cannot explain, for it is obviously more than difficult to be fully responsible and free in an absurd world. Sartrian man is not condemned to be Sysiphus; he chooses to be Sysiphus prepared to face life on the edge of despair. Could he choose to be something else? Not unless he could get rid of the absurdity of the world. Not only he cannot do that, but he knows that to entertain such a possibility is an illusion which would make him live in bad faith; so, he accepts the absurdity of the world and his freedom at the same time. This attempt to reconcile, irreconcilable, is typical of Sartre's make-up.

Though he has apparently repudiated God, he can neither rid himself of Christian terminology and categories, nor has he been able to root the idea of God out of himself. The end of the first part of his autobiography entitled *Les Mots* is fully revealing of his attitude:

Je prétends sincèrement n'écrire que pour mon temps mais je m'agace de ma notoriété présente: ce n'est pas la gloire puisque je vis et cela suffit pourtant à démentir mes vieux rêves. Serait-ce que je les nourris encore secrètement? Pas tout a fait: je les ai, je crois, adaptés: puisque j'ai perdu mes chances de mourir inconnu, je me flatte quelquefois de vivre méconnu. Grisélidis pas morte. Pardaillan m'habite encore. Et Strogoff. Je ne relève que d'eux qui ne relèvent que de Dieu et je ne crois pas en Dieu. Allez vous y reconnaître. Pour ma part, je ne m'y reconnais pas et je me demande parfois si je ne joue pas à qui perd gagne et ne m'applique à piétiner mes espoirs d'autrefois pour que tout me soit rendu au centuple. En ce cas je serais Philoctète: magnifique et puant, cet infirme a donné jusqu'a son arc sans condition: mais, souterrainement, on peut être sûr qu'il attend sa récompense.

For Sartre, the true self, the essential self of man, if one can even dare to mention the notion of essence in connection with him, is freedom, and freedom is self-created. Yet, of course, even Sartrian men do not spring fully freedom-blessed out of nothingness; they all come from parents and grandparents, etc. and they are all involved in complex social patterns and historical situations which are bound to render Sartre's more or less transcendental freedom difficult to practise. This freedom is based upon a material body and upon a network of senses which entirely connect any given body with other bodies and with the universe; therefore its operations are much contaminated at the start by the trammels of the contingent world in which it is grounded. Sartre can of course carry out interesting demonstrations of his perfect freedom on the well-adjusted board of his imagination. Orestes, for instance, snubs off Jove, chides his remorse-laden sister, then shoulders up his newly won freedom and flies off into a vacuum. But this coruscating, transcendental Orestes, sprung not from Jove, whose authority he challenges, but from Sartre's atheistic head, is no relation at all of the Atrides, for if he were, he would unavoidably know the weight of his guilt and the burden of his family's bloody past, and he would duly revenge his father and go to the dogs, for a while at least, until Minerva and the Athenians are prepared to rescue him. If Sartrian Orestes, instead of having supposedly been born in Argos, thirty centuries ago, had been born in Paris or in London now, he couldn't possibly talk to his butcher, cobbler, or concierge in the way in which his creator makes him talk to Jove, for if so, he would go about with an empty belly and bare feet; and then he would not be free, he would have to call the doctor or die, of his free choice of course, and that could hardly be called leading a free life. With Sartre, the gods or God, have decidedly a bad time. If they exist, like Jove, he dismisses them, if they don't, like God who has been certified dead by Nietzsche, then that makes it that man is condemned to be free and to be responsible for everything he does, as if God's presence meant that He could be responsible for everything in life, from the moment a man ties his boots and faces his porridge in the morning, to the moment he lays down his toothbrush and makes for his pillow at night. Sartrian Jove* is a kind of Valéryan Mephistopheles,† the plaything of the human intellect which chooses its actions without reference to anything or anybody. Electra, who has not been able to stand the strain of this terrifying freedom, collapses in the chains of her guilt and will be the prey of the Erinnies.

Sartre has explained that since society had accused Genet of being a thief, Genet had assumed the status which society offered him and had become a thief; yet he certainly knows that laws and commands do not relieve a man of his responsibilities; they, on the contrary, define them, and they give him a chance of avoiding to play at being God and making

---

* The Jove or Jupiter which Sartre created in *The Flies*.
† The character of Mephistopheles which Valéry created in *Mon Faust*.

everything, every time anew; they make it possible for man to act in solidarity with other men and to bend his will or his freedom to certain patterns which we might call values, and which are what men make them. Racing a horse to fetch a doctor for a dying man is a valuable action, racing the same horse in the entrails of the earth in order to carry coal so as to increase the ill-gotten gains of the horse's owner is a mean, heartless action. Sartre's philosophy bristles with difficulties, but he leaps gaily over them and, shunning the common lot of human kind, presents us with generally extraordinary men or extraordinary situations in which a human being stakes his whole life on his actions and tensions. These moments are necessarily dramatic in the sense that they are packed with emotions, and they reveal the very essence of the human beings involved. The three characters of *Huis Clos* are caught in a moment which reveals their true identity, and therefore pins them for ever on to the eternal. Once they have been laid naked through one of Sartre's most accomplished dramatic actions, they can only echo Garcin's final words: "Well, let's continue!" The atmosphere is Ibsenian, and the elimination of the division into acts renders this play as taut as Strindberg's *Miss Julie*, and shows Sartre to be a master craftsman and a sound psychologist.

The drama of ideas is, by its nature, always on the verge of melodrama, but Sartre can tread the boundary line between the two with great skill and he no sooner finds himself for a brief moment on the wrong side, than he is swept back into drama by a tide of overwhelming emotions. His ideas find their way in his plays, but they never turn into abstractions. *Huis Clos* sets about to show that hell is the others and that man is what the others think he is, but the conflict of the human beings involved in this demonstration is carried out through flesh and blood and not through abstractions or hollow rhetoric. Sartre always rises from a naturalistic framework and order towards essential truths. He is as much concerned with the inner self as Maeterlinck, but his search for the inner self is in the opposite direction of that of Maeterlinck. Instead of isolating the soul in a mystery world of anguishes and silence, Sartre connects it with the world and with the society in which it lives, thus following the Ibsenian pattern upon which he has grafted his existentialist preoccupations. For instance, the main question of *Les Mains Sales* is not why Hugo killed Hoederer, something which provides a good deal of excitement, but what will Hugo make of his deed. That question can only be solved once he has become fully aware of the fate which confronts him. At that point, he decides to give to his own death and to that of Hoederer the meaning which, according to him, they ought to have. In *Le Diable et le Bon Dieu*, Goetz tries in vain to be the absolutely good, fails and decides to give to his life and death the meaning which they ought to have. Franz and his father, obsessed by a guilt which is that of their family and also of their country, in the play *Les Séquestrés de l'Altona* which shows Sartre's dramatic talents at their best, come to the same conclusion and put an end to their *mauvaise foi*, through death. Sartre is all the more likeable because of his human contradictions, his love of men and his undeniable creative genius. His work testifies to this latter assertion and his life shows that he has honesty, integrity and courage. Few would have devoted as much energy as he has to defend St. Genet and other under-dogs, and fewer still would have taken the risks which he has taken. So, long may he go on writing plays, novels and philosophy and preaching and contradicting his preachings.

His ethical pronouncements stress the fact that man must shoulder his own responsibility, without the protection of conventions—social or otherwise—including the protection of religious principles. Man must look into his conscience, face up to his doubts and reach the verge of despair before he can hope to get on the other side. We are back to Pascal, Luther, Kierkegaard and all those who have to confront the world around them with their naked consciences and without any dogmatism to protect them, not even that of reason. "Whoever wants to be a Christian", said Luther, "should tear the eyes out of his reason . . . one must part with reason and not know anything of it and even kill it, else one will not get into the Kingdom of Heaven." The man who is

looking for God must go through the night of unknowing
and face nothingness and despair. From Augustine to St. John
of the Cross, Pascal, Luther or Kierkegaard, all the great lights
which illumine the road of the search for God have done so in
doubts, despair and total surrender of self to the call which
God made upon them.

Claudel wrote all his plays before the second world war, yet
his reputation as a dramatist can be said to be only two
decades old, and is mostly due to the untiring efforts of Jean-
Louis Barrault whose productions of *Le Soulier de Satin* and
Christophe Colomb are among the most outstanding theatrical
events of the last two decades. Barrault proved that Claudel
was not only a major poetic genius but an important poet-
dramatist. Claudel's drama is part of his religious universe
and his Christian vision of the world. For him, life is continuous conflict between good and evil, God and Satan,
ignorance and conscience and is therefore naturally dramatic.
Drama for him, is like Greek drama—religious, and he has
done more than anybody else to create a religious theatre.
Claudel's precocious genius came to grips very young with the
main themes which he sought to explore throughout his life;
they are the themes of a very devout Christian. *Tête d'or*,
which is his first play, contains them all; they are pride, con-
quest, faith and grace through evil and suffering, for evil is
part of creation. *L'échange* and *Partage de Midi* illustrate
these same themes in a dramatic poetry, the beauty of which
had not been equalled on the French stage since Racine. *La
Jeune Fille Violaine*, which became *L'Annonce faite à
Marie*, is one of the greatest miracle-plays of the world theatre.
Claudel's imagination went on widening its range, and if
Le Soulier de Satin is, as far as drama is concerned, something
which only Barrault's skill and ingenuity succeeded in com-
pressing into a stageable version which lasted nevertheless
five hours, it is undeniably a work of genius and a great work.
The scene is the world, the moment is that in which Catholicism embraces the cosmos and pervades all human actions
whether they are for or against it. In this cosmos torn by conflicts, the fate of two outstanding human beings destined to

each other from all eternity, yet separated by contingencies which they must respect, impinges upon all things. Rodrigue the conqueror, the discoverer of new lands for God, and Prouhèze the noble woman, meant to be his star in heaven and destined to him since timelessness, must nevertheless tear out their love from their human hearts, so that their eternal love might live. What complexities, and how mysterious the God who ordered them! Yet there they are, and these two crucified lovers must tread their tortuous, sorrowful paths, criss-crossed with necessary evil, so that their purity might, in the end, be rewarded. Prouhèze, at a certain moment, a widow, could have married Rodrigue who was also free, but she, on the contrary married Camille who is a self-conscious incarnation of evil, and has from him a daughter who is as much a spiritual daughter of Rodrigue as Mara's child was a spiritual daughter of her saintly sister Violaine. Camille needs Prouhèze more than Rodrigue, not because he loves her, but because he is damned, and Prouhèze must save him at the price of her earthly happiness, and she has to do so because it is only once she has carried this absolute surrender of her humanity, that she will be fit to be Rodrigue's star. How can one fathom the strange mysteriousness of God's ways! What do they mean? Is existential love incompatible with spiritual love! But then, why should two human beings be dedicated to each other from eternity? Or is it because God requires total obedience and surrender, and that the greater, the more heart-rending the earthly attachment to be shed, the greater the rise! Is it in this sense that suffering and the loved woman or man are only God's hook to fish either of them or both up to heaven! It is no doubt an extraordinary conception, but Claudel was an extraordinary genius who has made a remarkable contribution to the idea of total theatre fostered by Antonin Arthaud and followed by Brecht. *Christophe Colomb*, with its music, ballet and film, is a sample of epic drama which anticipates Brecht. Claudel's mixture of pagan earthiness and full bloodedness with mystical Catholicism has resulted in a kind of baroque drama exemplified by *Le Soulier de Satin* in which sensuality and spirituality, music and dance commingle in an operatic splendour which embraces all the aspects of life. In this total drama or Calderonian comedy which is *Le Soulier de Satin*, all genres are mixed, farce and clowning jostle with profound seriousness, while the announcer every now and then makes it clear to the audience that they are watching a play and not trying to identify themselves with an apprehensible reality. The universe is God's great stage, and men are acting out their lives under the gaze of the divine Producer who will know what to do with each of them when the curtain falls. Claudel's dramatic pursuits are Miltonian; they are always attempts to uncover God's ways to men and God's love for men. Men cannot find God in Gadarene bliss or surfeited ignorance; they can only hope to discover Him with their own crowns of thorns on their foreheads and with the same abnegation and submission which His son had shown at the foot of the Cross. Man is not Christ; he is man, a compound of flesh and spirit, and the compound is the cause of conflicts, dramatic tensions and suffering. Flesh is sinful and it is only through suffering, acceptance of his plight and search for God that man can hope to reach timelessness.

The world of Montherlant, which must be briefly examined, carries no such metaphysical aura or aroma of spirituality. It is, above all, the world of man torn by internecine struggles, appetites and longings which belong to the domain of psychology. Montherlant is one of the few living dramatists who has a true sense of tragedy. His most important and successful plays like *La Reine Morte* and *Le Maître de Santiago* have the clear-cut ritualistic perfection of a bull fight. They deal with human beings at their moments of truth. During these moments, their merciless gaze plumbs their past and future and shows them their contradictions and frustrations and they react violently towards extremes; they try to shut out the world, like *Le Maître de Santiago*, or to shut out life, like Ferrante in *La Reine Morte*. Ferrante is full of pride and disappointed hopes; his son, through whom he had hoped to realise himself, is nowhere near the grandeur of which he had dreamt, and he who knows himself to be weak and vacillating, hates his son all the more for the palpable proof of his own failings and therefore seeks self-justification through his son's punishment and humiliation. He is cruel and emotional and plays with Inez like a cat with a mouse, and when she has shown that she trusts him, that she has moved him and proved his hatred wrong, he can only prove to himself that he is a strong man by having her killed. That he does, generating through the death of this pure, loving woman, a moment of noble, intense pathos which is as close to real tragedy as it has ever been in the modern theatre. Ferrante kills as priests killed their victims on the altar of their gods. Their ritualistic gesture was a means to exorcise evil and to wipe away sinfulness and corruption. Ferrante kills to exorcise himself. That is why this play of Montherlant seems to me to reach tragic stature, something which is Montherlant's most specific and important contribution to the contemporary theatre.

Jean Genet is with Samuel Beckett the most original dramatist of the post-war era. That does not mean that he has invented things unheard of before, something not possible in life and art which are continuous developments and contradictions and syntheses of what preceded. The nihilism, the revolt against society and conventions which one finds in Genet's play are part of the climate of his age and have deep roots. The aggressiveness of individuals, their isolation and obsessions with their own projects, go back to German idealism and are stock themes of the plays of Sartre who is a great admirer of Genet. The theatre as dream points to its Strindbergian ancestry, and the search for identity through masks and impersonations had been fully exploited by Pirandello. Genet has winnowed all these various ingredients through his striking poetic imagination and left upon them the distinct mark of his individuality. He is a kind of modern Villon without the sterling, unique genius of Villon; for although he has a good deal of imagination he cannot, like Villon, transmute reality into essence or free his poetic imagination from didacticism and sentimentality. Still he has undeniable poetic gifts, and while I should never dream of calling

Ionesco a poet, Genet is definitely one. His language rises from the page in beautiful images laden with meaning, and his invention is generally grounded in human realities. The private mythology of his characters is always based on sound psychological and social reasons. Society made of Genet a thief and, as Sartre puts it, Genet decided to be what society wanted him to be. Society makes of some men outcasts and these men take to dreams and myth-making. Society treats some as convicts, slaves, prisoners without meaning or influence, in fact as objects, and these objects retire underground, in their dream world and either ignore or try to destroy society. Genet is a bolder, delinquent Mallarmé; instead of sheltering behind esotericism, he sends his poet-criminals into a brothel where they live their illusions for the duration of a dream, and then go back to life. The chief of police of his most famous play *Le Balcon* has not yet become the subject of erotic impersonations; therefore he is not yet part of myth like bishops and generals. Life is a naked struggle for power and sex is one of the means to achieve it; that is why a brothel is a house of illusions. The revolution which forms the background of this play does not really merge with the obsessions of the main protagonists and is on the whole rather extraneous to them. The only connection between the two is that the revolutionary leaders also need myths and illusions and so they turn the beautiful prostitute Chantal into a mythical, sexual symbol so as to enthuse the revolutionaries into action.

Once she is killed the bishop canonises her. The chief of police opposes the revolution as befits a chief of police and anxiously watches the brothel, waiting for the consecration of his power and influence in society. The chief of the revolution realises, while trying to impersonate the chief of police, that he too is craving for power; so he castrates himself in order to punish himself and by sympathetic magic the chief of police, who has chosen as an emblem a gigantic phallus. This action is the sign that the chief of police has at last entered the world of myth and of men's dreams of sex and power. *Le Balcon* has its flaws and its incoherences, but it remains a powerful and memorable play, and Genet's best contribution to the modern theatre. Genet is not concerned with absurdity in any form, he is concerned with individual identity, social ostracism and redress, and with the theatre as ritual and as means to turn life into a game. His characters are completely non-naturalistic, their impersonations, symbolic appearances and metaphors are reflections in mirrors which have taken the place of the real world.

Ionesco's world is completely different. His fantasies, which in my view never rise to the imaginative transmutations of Genet, are generally grounded into naturalistic settings and backgrounds with which they do not merge. The result is fantasy without wisdom or emotional power and a type of comic which can only be taken in small drafts, if not it becomes inane, repetitious and boring. The allegories are too cardboardy, too fustian to be taken seriously or with interest by the modern world which is used to confining such dramatic means to the medieval stage or to the nursery and the world of early childhood. The allegory of Amedée's corpse is too crude, too childish to be accepted, except as a joke; so is that of men turning into rhinoceroses and so is the expressionism of *Tueur sans Gages* or the three noses of Jacques's fiancée. These are the kind of fantasies which may pass muster in an evening at the music-hall, but to call them poetic transmutations is to call a cow's horn a newly born moon. They may look alike from a distance, but they only share one trait— their semicircular shape. In a similar way, Ionesco's fantasies have at times one quality which pertains to poetry and which is the element of surprise; but of course, it is not the quality which makes the entity.

Ionesco's theatre is the mirror of an incoherent meaningless world, which, indulging in the mimetic fallacy, is itself often incoherent and utterly boring. The attempt to convey boredom, incoherence and incommunicability, mimetically or in their conceptualised forms, rests upon a self-contradictory foundation. It is obvious that if life were as utterly boring and incoherent as Ionesco and those who label it absurd believe it to be, it could neither be transmuted into art, nor would it be worth while trying to do so. Anyone who truly believes in life's absurdity can only leave every man to his own impenetrable absurd world without attempting the impossible and at the same time contradicting his own beliefs. The logic of such beliefs would be silence and not loquacity and claims to public attention. It is therefore obvious that Ionesco's belief in the absurdity and incoherence of life are both circumscribed to certain sections of life and are in many cases the result of social conventions and beliefs, which if modified would shed their detrimental effects. It is also obvious that Ionesco himself does not look upon himself and his work as fragments of the absurd world to which he is supposed to belong. He places himself outside this absurd world in order to laugh at it, and he hopes to find enough non-absurd readers or listeners to laugh with him at the absurdities which he describes, and to benefit from the cathartic effect of these experiences. All this means that the so-called priests of the absurd, whoever they are, should cast off any pretences at being the discoverers of a new, self-contradictory cult and recognise the fact that their notion of human absurdity and incoherence is as much a dramatic device as Molière's laughter at the Marquis, the Précieuses, the Hypocrites or the obsessed, like Harpagon or Oronte.

The incommunicability which is so much talked about is not a revelation of the twentieth century which has merely tried to systematise it. Men obsessed by their preoccupations, like Harpagon or others, followed their own trends of thoughts impervious to what happened around them. The important thing is that they were not as self-conscious, as is the case now, about their isolation. Besides that, the vital point is that the notion of incommunicability rests upon words and gestures which prepare the communicability or incommunicability of silence. People can only show that they do not understand one another by their words and their behaviour; without that, they do not know whether they connect or live and move in isolation. Therefore words still remain the most important means through which men can expound the incoherence, incommunicability or absurdity of their lives. One can only convey the lack of meaning through some kind of meaning which may convey the meaninglessness of the characters involved. Ionesco and his followers disclaim any use of traditional psychology, plot, and character sequence. Such notions postulate indeed a logic and coherence which they profess not to find in human life. So non-sense, non sequitur in behaviour and conversation are the dramatic means by which, according to them, one can show men's incoherence and isolation. There is no possible justification for logical behaviour, because obviously there are no values to which human behaviour can finally be referred to. Bérenger in *Tueur sans Gages* sets about to convince the killer of the uselessness of murder and ends in being compelled to admit that there is no reason not to kill, and that in fact, there is no reason for anything. In a world without categorical imperatives, humanistic or transcendental beliefs, all absurdities are given the same lack of importance, and life becomes a mixture of surrealistic fantasies and reality, as is so often the case in Ionesco's plays.

In *Tueur sans Gages*, the *"Cité radieuse"* is haunted by a maniac murderer who represents the forces of darkness opposed to the forces of sunlight and joy. The blend between these various aspects is inchoate and the play does not hold together. *Victimes du devoir* suffers from the same defect in that it is a mixture of surrealistic fantasy, psychoanalysis and didacticism. Guilt and the unredeemability of the past, which are so much part of Ibsen's world, are in *"Amédée,"* expressed not through human thoughts and emotions, but through the mechanical and artificial notion of a growing corpse and mushrooms. The world of Ionesco is a world of mechanicalness, artificiality and devices which are no doubt effective for farce, as part of a greater whole or when only used for a short time, but which become blunt and boring when they are abused. It is amusing to have every member of a family called Bobby Watson, and it is also amusing to have a conversation entirely made of clichés and platitudes about what everyone knows already, but the device breaks down when it is prolonged too far or is used throughout a whole play. There is a limit to the use of meaningless speeches, inane iterations and puns as means to portray the emptiness of the characters which make use of them. These characters offer no more interest than disembodied voices, and their boredom and incoherence is infectious and bores the audience. The only two plays in which Ionesco's devices are entirely successful are *The Chairs* which is his best play, and *The Lesson*. Both these plays carry a strong, human element which connects emotionally with the audience, in the case of *The Chairs* even more effectively than in the case of *The Lesson*. Writing about *The Chairs* Ionesco said: "The theme of this play is nothingness. . . . The invisible elements must be more and more clearly present until nothingness is heard, is made concrete."

The Chairs shows better than any other of Ionesco's plays the inanity of trying to communicate and the pathetic plight of two old people left in a desolate world, with only their dreams. The empty chairs vividly suggest the crowd which surrounds them and the iterations produce a definite, incantatory effect which goes to the heart. In *The Lesson* mechanicalness follows a kind of mathematical progression similar to that of *The Chairs* and ends in a frenzied rush and in one more murder. The movement of the play is very subtly engineered and is not without analogy with the sexual act. The theme is power, naturally connected with sex, and the teacher ends with what looks like sexual murder; after that, he calms down and takes up again his attitude of spoilt child under the control of his maid.

His theatre being the mirror of a meaningless world, and therefore meaningless, at least theoretically, Ionesco naturally professes a certain indifference to what the director does with his plays. For *Tueur sans Gages* he authorises "all cuts needed", for *L'Avenir est dans les œufs*, he offers various possibilities of ending the play. His stage directions generally aim at effects and not at defending the text. "Theatre is for me", says Ionesco, "the projection on the stages of the inner world. I reserve the right to take this theatrical material from my dreams, my obscure desires my inner contradictions." The material itself is held up to ridicule, its own contradictions and absurdities exposed. As he claims to have no message to deliver, though of course he is anything but free from didacticism and socio-psychological preachings the conclusions of his plays are generally negations and contradictions of what preceded so as to show clearly that all things are interchangeable, meaningless and absurd. On the other hand, Bérenger in *Rhinoceros*, ends the play with a violent protest that he will not surrender to conformity. That looks like something positive, although one can very well wonder how long Bérenger will be able to hold out against the pressure around him.

A theatre without psychology or plot, and without any attempts at characterisation and social truth is necessarily closely related to farce, and Ionesco has made full use of the mechanicalness of objects, of expressionism, masks and fantasies to create farcical situations in which human beings are sadly locked up in their isolation and anguish. It is a type of farce completely different from classical farce, which rested on caricatures and exaggerations of human traits and incongruous human situations which presupposed rationality and logic, and therefore laughter and human emotions. Ionesco's world is, on the contrary, a dehumanised world in which human beings are reduced to simple mechanical devices and allegories, all having exactly the same worth, which is no worth at all. This kind of lunatic, disjointed world can be entertaining for brief moments, but Ionesco's work to date proves that it cannot be so during three acts. Ionesco has fantastic invention but lacks the poetic imagination of dramatists like Brecht and Sartre whom he is quite prepared to denigrate; yet, without a good measure of such a gift, he will find it more difficult to sustain his rather inflated reputation.

S. Beckett's *Waiting for Godot* is the most original play of the post-war years. Here we are truly in the domain of imagination and poetry. We have no superficial allegories and personifications of abstractions, but characters who are both symbolic and real and a situation which is a metaphor of the human condition. The characters are all mankind, Abel and Cain, rich and poor, exploiter and exploited, dying or living astride their already prepared grave, and waiting like all men, for the revelation of the mystery which is not dead but absconded and keeps their souls and lives in suspense. This is the true metaphysical, Pascalian and Kierkegaardian absurdity and nonsense of life without God or without purpose, and it is something which is very remote from the dehumanised, incoherent world of Ionesco. The anguish of *Godot* is not the anguish of the void but the anguish of absence; it is certainly closer to the anguish of Sartrian freedom which is as much a categorical imperative as if freedom, instead of being purely an immanent value, were also transcendent.

The truth is that it is impossible to posit immanence without some form of transcendence, at least in abeyance; therefore the malediction which weighs upon Goetz, Sartre's play *Le Diable et le Bon Dieu*, together with his Satanism and challenge to God, are religious notions which endow this play with far-reaching metaphysical reverberations and profound human truth. *Waiting for Godot* bathes in a metaphysical atmosphere which excludes expressionism, abstractions and allegories. Objects like the tree, the hat and the shoes carry symbolic connotations, while even the apparent philosophising of the tramps is fully integrated in the play as a means of exteriorising their feelings and the awareness of their condition. While the words poetry and poems are so lightly bandied about in connection with the modern stage that they are often meaningless, *Waiting for Godot* is a poem and for reasons very different from those generally invoked when the word poetry is used in connection with certain fashionable contemporary dramatists. The first one is that its reality must be experienced as a whole, because the play attempts to mirror the wholeness of life. It is a poem, and it is essentially a symbolist poem, in the direct line of Maeterlinck's drama. The action only progresses in the sense that there are two acts which require a certain amount of sequential time for performance, but there is in fact no dramatic progression or tension. The action is static, confined to waiting for something which is never clearly defined. Waiting is a condition of human kind and those who wait use words as in Maeterlinck's plays, not to construct or defeat arguments, but to keep their anguish at bay and to give meaning and creativeness to silence.

The play is not perfect, the second act lacking, of necessity, the originality of the first; this was very much less noticeable in the English production, which was altogether better than the French, which was too naturalistic. The first act is a masterpiece and the most original piece of dramatic writing of the last twenty years. Beckett has carried to a successful and final conclusion a type of Maeterlinckian drama which cannot be repeated, since he has been able to dramatise in that form the very plight of the human condition. *End Game*, *Krapp's Last Tape* and *Embers* are nothing more than continuations, or shreds and left overs from the great theme which he explored in *Waiting for Godot*. That is why all imitations are futile and are as much parodies as attempts to imitate *Hamlet* or the *Mona Lisa*. One may add moustaches to her, or dress her up as a modern fashion model; the result is merely a condemnation of the one who attempts it, for the fact is that once a theme has been fully explored by genius, only a genius of superior calibre could add something to it. Beckett's universal, tragic farce which is connected with the writings of other Irish playwrights like Synge and O'Casey is a mirror of modern life which follows and completes the picture of it presented by *The Waste Land* at the end of the first world war. Time, in Beckett as well as in Eliot, is not sequential time, but time lived; it is the Bergsonian duration. Time, in *Godot*, is meaningless because of the absence of transcendence which confers meaning upon it.

The play takes place during two evenings which seem at one point to be two different seasons, since in the second evening, the tree, by which the action takes place, bears leaves. Although the tree being symbolical of the hanging tree, its bearing of leaves could, of course, be a symbolic sign of the hope which makes it possible for the two tramps to go on waiting. The tree is also the solitary tree of the Noh plays, which Yeats admired and sought to emulate. Life measured by the standards of eternity is *one* day; "one day we are born, one day we die, we live astride a grave". All things are the same since they lack their real meaning which is the reason for which the two tramps are waiting. Didi and Gogo, Ham and Clov are meaningless, and life is a tale told by an idiot; but all this is due not to inherent absurdity, but to an absence of meaning. The tramps are complex creatures with various levels of meaning which range from the particular to the universal. At one level, they are well-defined, Chaplinesque figures done down by life and carrying clear-cut naturalistic attributes which they share with that category of tramps. At the other level, they are no ordinary tramps; they are, on the contrary, two extremely singular tramps since they stand for something more than their own appearance in that they are the bearers of the most important aspects of the self-consciousness of man; they carry with them the metaphysical awareness and the anxiety of absence, and they are waiting, waiting for the true meaning of life.

Their language, loaded with meaning, suggestiveness and ambiguities, is both a poetic and a continuously dramatic language in the sense that it is never used for its own sake, but always in order to develop the dramatic situation in which they find themselves. Their gestures, their clownish tricks, their hunger, fears, quarrels and bad faith are practically all referential and symbolic; so are the dialectical permutations of Lucky and Pozzo who represent the master–slave, rich and poor, stupid and intelligent, exploiter and exploited relationship. The two tramps Vladimir and Estragon are real in the way Alceste of Molière is real; they are recognisable and highly singularised tramps, each one with his own habits, feelings and reactions, and they are also types, representing a whole aspect of human kind. They are real, they eat, sleep, squabble, are slapped and beaten by others, and they suffer and they are in a situation which is that of the human condition. They are waiting for a strange entity called Godot, and they stand for human kind aware of transcendence and waiting for a sign of its presence. We have here no incoherent mixture of fancy and naturalism as in Ionesco; we have, on the contrary, a striking example of the dramatic embodiment of true realism in which every aspect of phenomenal appearance is informed with substance and is symbolic of true reality.

The setting of the play is the earth, practically anywhere; it is sufficiently nondescript to be so, and it fits with the lack of exact biographical details about the two tramps who could belong to any nationality. They don't quite know whence they came, and their social background is of no importance; they neither remember their past clearly nor the exact reasons why they are where they are, and of course, the lack of precision about their social origins only serves to emphasise their true humanity. The vague stages and actions they have gone through perfectly apply to mankind in general. They have been more prosperous and happier in the past, they had hopes and inspiration, and Estragon was a poet; they gathered crops together, they ran risks together; Vladimir even fished Estragon out of the Durance, and that is a very concrete fact.

They have had ups and downs, but it is obvious that life has been, up till now, worth living. They are neither interchangeable nor are they social types like the characters of social realistic drama; they are two individuals who embody various fundamental aspects of mankind. First, they embody the masculine and the feminine. Vladimir, who is more active, more restless, more intellectualised, is the masculine; Estragon, who is more spontaneous, more childlike, more egotistical, more obstinate, more prone to moods and in need of protection, is the feminine. He is also the victim, he is kicked by Lucky; he has even tried to commit suicide; he is jealous, easily angered, and he reproaches Vladimir for singing in his absence. He threatens to go away and does not, and he is as much tied to Vladimir as some married couples are tied to each other by their respective inability to live apart. The two tramps need each other, have affection for each other, and although their quarrelling is at times comical like all quarrelling, they can't part and they have compassion and love for each other. They are two archetypal heroes or characters as much detached from any social historical context as Alceste, Phèdre, or Hamlet; they have no direct influence upon society's economy and politics; they are in fact not in a social situation circumscribed by a function or by loyalty to a social group—proletarian or bourgeois, they are in the human situation. They are a metaphor of the human condition and represent what is unchanging and what transcends the particular and the socio-historical aspect of human life. They are man in solitude, yet desperately trying to get out of it, and sometimes succeeding, but more often failing in the two most fundamental aspects of human life, which are that man can neither share his sorrows and suffering nor his death. Whatever Godot is, it is obvious that the two tramps, like other men, can only get out of their solitude through God, for togetherness is a religious experience. Here God is in a suspended state of absence and Vladimir and Estragon are in a state of continuous agitation because they cannot face up to the solitude which threatens them. They know the cause of their vain agitation and suffering, yet they go on, because there is nothing else that they can do. Suicide is too positive an act, and as they have not resolved their contradictions they are not in a position to take such a positive step. When they try, the rope breaks; still, they go on thinking about it, and the play ends with Vladimir saying that they will hang the following day. But that is unlikely, Estragon has his trousers down and cannot move, so they say; let's go, but do not move. Their apathy and natural aptitude to wait are against it, and above all, the hope that Godot might turn up is never entirely given up.

Pozzo and Lucky are society, and they are a world completely alien to that of the two tramps. Pozzo is the master and Lucky is the slave, laden with burdens, tied to him by a rope. The Pozzo–Lucky relationship is the mirror of human degradation and shallowness. Pozzo hides his insignificance and hollowness under a cloak of ritual gestures and ceremonies which are part of the social apparatus of power. In the second act, Pozzo is blind and entirely at the mercy of his slave who now leads him with a rope which has been considerably shortened. At this stage, they encounter again the tramps and they all tumble down in general confusion and try again to get up but without success, as is the case with humankind without God. Pozzo's life is appearance without substance; his life is what he owns, and Lucky is part of it. Lucky is merely an object, a thing, and his life is reduced to mechanical reactions; he not only serves Pozzo, he also has to think for him; he is therefore materially and spiritually Pozzo's slave and has no individual existence. His incoherent speech at his Master's bidding is a brilliant illustration of the subservience and menial position of the intellectual and the artist in a society composed of Pozzos. The final outcome of this type of servitude is delirium and silence.

If the situation of the two tramps is that of the human condition, and therefore something which transcends socio-historical time, that of Pozzo and Lucky, who are social beings, is entirely subjected to the laws of time. They change from one day to another; Vladimir notes this change and Estragon acknowledges it with the words: "Very likely; they all change, only we can't." The two tramps can't change because time for them has stopped; they are suspended upon the moment of expectancy which represents now and always the very core of the human condition. Pozzo and Lucky, who do not even have a glimmer of the idea of transcendence, are merely part of the contingent world; they represent society at its last gasp, dying of the master–slave relationship. Lucky who, before, could dance, could therefore do something creative, now can only relieve his master's boredom through his intellectual delirium. Soon society will be entirely composed of blind masters and mute slaves, or of partially paralysed, half-frozen men like Ham and Clov in *Fin de Partie (End Game)*. Pozzo fears change; he wants to remain what he is—a wealthy well-fed owner of slaves; but this cannot be done. Time moves on and necessarily brings about its dialectical deteriorations. This is historical time, and up to a point, Marx's time with its inexorable dialectics. The time of the tramps is Baudelaire's time, the time of endless 'taedium" and metaphysical anxiety. Nothing happens, nothing changes, and all attempts to act in order to bring about change are vain, for action, having lost its sacramental value, is merely an empty gesture like those taking place in Pozzo's and Lucky's world where everything is purely contingent. There, all actions are illusions to keep at bay the awareness of illusion.

Whatever happens in *Waiting for Godot* is like the negative of a film; it is something which can only exist if it is developed and brought to light by the positive intervention of the photographer. In the play, action could only be made positive by the appearance of Godot whose absence fills the waiting and negates everything that takes place in this atmosphere of waiting which is a vacuum. Nothing positive could take place in such an atmosphere, since no action could coincide with its purpose which, in this case, does not exist. All the actions are dependent upon waiting for Godot or for God whose absence causes the vacuum of waiting and negates everything, including the tramps' hunger, suffering and fears. Hunger and fear are real enough; they are experienced both physically and mentally, but as they take place in a world from which all meanings have been absolutely sucked out by, and dissolved into, the absence which the tramps are waiting and longing for, these phenomenal happenings, although real, have no meaning. They could only acquire meaning through the appearance of Godot, that is to say through a positive belief in God. Without His appearance or, to be precise, without His existence, life, instead of being as it is—bi-polarised between Being and non-being, is merely non-being and meaninglessness, or if one likes, absurd, although a very definite type of absurdity. It is, in this context, the absurdity of non-being, that is to say something which can have no reality until the emergence of Being. It is only within Being that non-being can be posited, and in this case the absurdity attached to it is not the absurdity of an atheistic, incoherent world, but the absurdity of the subjective judgments of those who, unable to find a meaning to creation, refuse to accept the unavoidable margin of irrationality and mystery which necessarily pertains to transcendence, and which divides the finite from the infinite.

The absurdity of the atheist is objective absurdity which can only be meaningless and devoid of any hope, since it is looked upon as pure contingence without any informing substance, therefore without any hope of change. It is condemned to be eternally what it is; it is like Sartre's Hell. In it, men will always be what they are, endlessly repeating the same meaningless, mechanical gestures which are like phantasmic gestures without real existence, or like the limbo world of Nietzsche's eternal cycles. This view of absurdity can be entertained as a dramatic device, or as a kind of intellectual, protective shell, forbidding questioning and metaphysical anxiety, but this very lack of metaphysical anxiety makes it intellectually untenable; for, as previously noted, it turns a concept—that of absurdity—into an absolute. There lies the fundamental difference between the concept of the absurd of Ionesco and Co. and that of Beckett, which is also that of Pascal and Kierkegaard. These two attitudes have nothing in common, except a name. The world of Beckett is only absurd and meaningless because of the absence of Godot. That of Ionesco is just plain incoherent, mechanical and riddled with fantasies and nightmares, and lacking a centre which is the self-awareness of absence. It is a world of soap-bubbles and purely contingent phenomena. The absurd in this case is an emotional state in which the writer, as comfortably ensconced in it as a mouse in a Dutch cheese, makes full use of the world, while at the same time rejecting it as absurd. He declares that life is absurd and shorn of any affective or rational logic, or that men are unable to communicate, and yet, in spite of that he insists in attempting to share this absurdity and this incommunicability with his fellow beings.

This is part and parcel of the paradox of modern life. On the one hand, God has been duly certified dead, on the other, the modern atheist, instead of partaking in the liberating joy of his eighteenth-century rationalist forebears, behaves like a child who has been forsaken by his parents and either desperately tries, as Nietzsche did, to put himself in God's place or ends, as Sartre does, in worshipping the void or nothingness left behind by God's absence. Nietzsche was too great a genius and had too much lucidity to finally delude himself about "man, presumptuous sample of the animal species, whose life is happily measured". Sartre, on the contrary, does delude himself when he tries to make his freedom spontaneously surge out of nothingness, which thus becomes the ground of being. With such a ground, existence can only be incoherent, absurd, nightmarish or a kind of allegory without meaning, since the true, informing substance of life has been replaced by transcendental nothingness. A world based on transcendental nothingness has no place for true realism and particularism; it can only offer materialism and abstraction. This is the case of Ionesco. Sartre avoids these pitfalls through his imagination, his deep psychological insight, his social zeal and his humanism which contradict some of his philosophical tenets.

The world of Beckett is not allegorical but symbolic; it rests not on transcendental nothingness, but on absent transcendence, and on an objective embodiment of certain aspects of modern life. Yet, in spite of this objectivity it remains on the whole a subjective, rather static, non-dynamic, practically non-historical world, in the sense that, although his characters are vaguely aware of their past, they live in a negativated present and have no future. The kernel of realism which, transmuted by imagination, is the basis of the greatness of *Godot*, remains a frozen, fixed point in time. It offers a profoundly true picture of man, but it is man already partially caught in spreading ice while the earth itself is being slowly covered by it; it is therefore a terrifying picture of man under the looming threat of fossilisation. Lear also has to go through barrenness, icy lands and night, but he is always fully alive, with a past, a present and a finality which give meaning to his death and to that of Cordelia. This meaning is that, far from being the plaything of a blind, absurd fate, nothing in life happens which is not part of historical and eschatological orders which can only be mediated through man's vision, suffering and greatness. The Shakespearian world is objective, true to reality as apprehended through imagination, dynamic, coherent and part of a greater whole implying a finality and justice which preclude absurdity. The world of *Waiting for Godot* could not be described in such terms, its reality, instead of being part of a whole, tends on the contrary to be the whole, which is reduced to an image of nihilism and moving despair within the context of absent transcendence.

Godot, of course, is not specifically God, although his vague attributes could fit any powerful master. His behaviour is unpredictable; he treats well the boy who minds the goats, and beats without reason the one who minds the sheep. He could bring joy or tears, and Estragon fears his arrival. Pozzo answers both to the names of Abel and Cain when Estragon calls him. The tramps compare themselves to the two thieves hanged upon the cross, and they wonder if one of them might be saved. The tree upon which they propose to hang is very much a hanging cross. The waiting of the two tramps is not the waiting for a definite human being; it is obviously the waiting for something more. Since waiting is their whole life, nothing else matters, except the anxiety to fill the vacuum caused by the absence of Godot, so their waiting inescapably is a parable of the human condition. "We are not saints; but we have kept our appointment. How many people can boast as much?", says Didi; and Gogo significantly answers: "Billions."

Beckett's other plays repeat, emphasise and continue to its logical end, certain aspects of *Godot*'s theme. Ham, with his parents already half-dead and confined to dustbins, and Clov no longer wait for Godot. It is too late; the dreaded catastrophe has already taken place. They are practically the sole survivors, with the exception of a man and his son whom life will soon exterminate. They wait for the end of life and for the earth to freeze into immobility. Maimed and half-paralysed, they consciously play the game of living, and at the fall of the final curtain which Ham—actor, Hamlet, fallen prince—rings down by putting his handkerchief on his face, the game is over, the last gasps of the human condition have come to an end. Henceforth all will be silence. All the characters of Beckett's plays are aware that they are on the stage, and sometimes they address the audience directly. Ham in *Fin de Partie* tries to perform certain numbers, and, like Lucky, he comments about his performance. Beckett's characters share with those of Anouilh and Genet the notion that the theatre is a game, that life itself is a game, and a game worth playing, without nevertheless taking it too seriously. *Godot*'s tramps are always aware that they are both actors and spectators. Life is like the theatre, a let-us-pretend game, and it has often been described as a stage upon which men perform their tricks. The material world, which Sartre described as the world of viscosity, is either hostile, or at least not attuned to the human. Shoes and hats are too small, trousers too large, windows too high and ropes easily break; the objects, in fact, refuse to co-operate with the humans. The shoes and the bowler hat enable *Godot*'s tramps to play a real vaudeville act, very reminiscent of the world of Charlie Chaplin who is, by now, one of the widely accepted myths of modern man. Both tramps emulate Chaplin in dress and manners; their hats, shoes, their way of kicking are pure Chaplin, and so is their insistence on the importance of little things.

Life is a game which never ends and man is always conscious of its absurd brevity. "The end is in the beginning", says Ham, parodying T. S. Eliot. Life is a brief play performed for nothing, yet the only one men have a chance to play in, so they might as well go on with the performance as long as it lasts. Mrs. Rooney dreams of annihilation and continues to enjoy the landscape; Ham and Clov call for the end, yet they continue to play the game of the man who cannot sit down and the one who cannot get up. Beckett's characters are always two by two, including Willie and Winnie, in his latest play *Happy Days*. Krapp himself has his recorded voice which is his other self. Each character needs the other to play with, or to bounce against and to express the ups and downs of existence. The ties which keep these various couples together do not transform them or give them happiness, yet they cannot be dissolved. They squabble and threaten, they shout and complain but they never forget that they are necessary to each other; they are in many ways Chekovian, they hug and struggle and they indulge in emotions. They try to communicate and sometimes, as is the case with the two tramps in *Godot*, they succeed, but Lucky and Pozzo can't. Their master–slave relation makes communication impossible.

Beckett's vision of man is that of a forlorn species in a more or less advanced state of decay and approaching final paralysis. In *Fin de Partie*, the characters are confined to their respective dustbins; "to hell with the universe", says Ham. Life has nearly reached its last stage. *Krapp's Last Tape* takes place in a shadowy hole, and Winnie, in *Happy Days*, is buried in a mound of earth up to the neck. Final silence is near, Pozzo dreams of annihilation and wonders if he is not asleep. Beckett has succeeded in dramatising one of the main aspects of the human condition and in turning it into a symbolic entity in which its component parts—the characters—have a universal validity. The word "poet" is too liberally used and is sometimes applied to writers who obviously confuse fancy and imagination, verbal decorations and poetry. Beckett is a poet and his imagination transmutes reality into a super-reality which has a universal meaning. His language is always precise and with subtle rhythms which convey a wide range of human attributes. It moves from the apparent incoherence of Lucky to the violent shouts of Pozzo or the puns, clichés and double-meanings of the tramps. It can both communicate and show the incapacity to communicate or the threat of disintegration, and by so doing it shows of course its vitality, while the poet himself shows his artistry and mastery. Beckett's words can act as a screen behind which lurk ignorance and incomprehension, or as a noise to keep at bay the fear of the dark and silence. Above all, they can suggest what logic and reason cannot express, and as such, they are part of a truly symbolist poem in which language is not only a means of describing and making statements, but is the very being of the poem. *Waiting for Godot* is an achievement of a high order and the epigoni who try to emulate it without Beckett's poetic insight cannot but fall back on concepts and abstractions which only serve to underline the high standards and excellence of the original.

CHAPTER FOUR

POETIC DRAMA

ANY attempt to unravel the particular or significant British and American contribution to contemporary drama is unfailingly brought face to face with the sharp cleavage, which is more marked in Britain than in America, between poetic drama and prose drama. The expression "poetic drama" has now acquired a distinctly effete and pejorative meaning which, in most cases, automatically disqualifies it from competing on equal terms with other forms of drama. The fashion for poetic drama has ebbed away with the emotional tidal wave of the war and with the coming of age of the new generation of theatre-goers, reared in the welfare state, impatient with the past and tossed between sensationalism, self-generated grievances and the anxieties of a very uncertain future. The new fashion is for social naturalism and for the so-called theatre of the absurd. As naturalism is a contaminated word which no one would dare to parade as a reputable banner, it is very often replaced by the words realism, poetic naturalism—a very strange marriage indeed—or by poetic realism, something to be welcomed and admired, if only it were an expression of the truth. Yet of course poetic drama is anything but dead and buried, and whether one circumscribes its meaning to the verse drama of Lorca, Claudel, Yeats, Eliot, MacLeish and Fry or whether one includes the poetic realism of O'Neill, Synge, O'Casey and Beckett, all Irish, it remains, all in all, the most striking and important aspects, not only of contemporary drama, but of the last half-century. Verse drama is above all a technical term which it seems difficult fully to equate with poetic drama. One shudders at the exiguity of its meshes which would not let through most of Ibsen's or Synge's drama, so

6

mention only two, and which would compel Claudel to produce serious credentials for his "verset". We are happily
spared an arduous excursion through academic brushwoods
by the limitations of the subject of this enquiry which is
about the works of contemporary playwrights which are being
performed now, that is to say during the last decade or so.
This kind of delineation excludes Yeats, a great poet, and an
important dramatist whose work will one day be given its due
recognition. Shunning the debate between prose and verse
which is unnecessary, since the field of prose drama will be
briefly examined later, and bearing in mind the fact that the
hostility against poetic drama is really directed against verse
drama, the question resolves itself into trying to find out
whether or not verse drama has made any worth-while contribution to drama as a whole.

This question is certainly not new; it began to trouble
poets as soon as they became aware that verse was no longer
the accepted medium of artistic expression, as soon, in fact
as it began to sound unnatural. "J'avoue", said Corneille,
"que les vers que l'on récite sur le théâtre sont présumés
être prose; nous ne parlons pas d'ordinaire en vers et sans
cette fiction, leur mesure et leur rime sortiraient du vrai-
semblable. . . . Il faut se servir au théâtre de vers qui sont les
moins vers et qui se mêlent au langage commun, sans y penser
plus souvent que les autres." The rhythm of the Alexandrine,
which is determined more by the rhetoric of the emotions
than by strict prosodic rules, can certainly move side by side
with prose and rise to poetry whenever it is charged with
emotional power. Racine's example proves it, and Racine
wrote the kind of transparent, fluid and pliable verse which
is first and foremost an instrument of drama. The iambic
pentameter is also very close to prose rhythms and it can
move side by side with it, with a perfect air of naturalness, or
rise on the wings of metaphors and images, whenever necessary. The main point of Elizabethan drama and of the French
classical age is that the leading dramatis personae were
generally characters of noble birth, who were therefore
expected to use an elevated style of expression. Another im-

portant point was that the audience was used to verse. This soon changed; tragedy gave way to melodrama and *drame bourgeois*, verse to prose as a means of literary expression, and by the nineteenth century, verse was no longer the accepted medium of dramatic expression for a public more and more used to prose. Ibsen thought that "verse had been injurious to dramatic art and that the aims of the dramatist of the future were almost certain to be incompatible with it". Maeterlinck understood the lesson and sought to produce poetic drama, not by writing in verse, but by concentrating upon poetic themes and situations, and by creating, through gestures and silences, an atmosphere of poetry which not only did not need verse, but sought to do away with the words themselves which he replaced by whispers, sighs and silences. "On peut affirmer que le poème se rapproche de la beauté et d'une vérité supérieure, dans la mesure où il élimine les paroles qui expliquent les actes pour les remplacer par des paroles qui expliquent non pas ce qu'on appelle 'un état d'âme', mais je ne sais quels efforts insaisissables et incessants des âmes vers leur beauté et vers leur vérité." Maeterlinck obviously rejoins Wagner and points to the mood play which is a development of symbolist poetry which was much favoured by Yeats, and is also one of the important features of modern drama.

Yeats was as much concerned as Mallarmé, Verlaine or Villiers de l'Isle-Adam with keeping an appropriate distance from life. A play, for him as well as for Maeterlinck, was a poem to be apprehended as a whole and not through any structure of plot and character. A play, like a poem, is more what it is than what it says; it does not instruct or moralise, it imparts wisdom through active participation in a creative experience. Like a symbolist poem, the play moves from the real to its transmutation into essential images which embody reality in movement as if it were a highly stylised dance. The poem and the play are both a kind of dance, a duration which can only be lived through creativeness. That is why Yeats found such deep affinities with the Noh plays with their non-naturalistic scenery and their chanting chorus-musicians; that is why he used dancers, music and masks to rise to essential reality. But if Yeats's early phase of Celtic dreaminess and shadowy waters is akin in some ways to the Mallarmean refusal of the world, Yeats's eroticism, rooted in the body, was very remote from Mallarmé's intellectual eroticism, love of abstractions and search for transcendence. For Yeats, Hérodiade's frozen virginity has to descend into the mire of passion, for the body needs to have its say, and, of course, it cannot have it through the heady dreams of fauns. Besides that, he was passionately devoted to the cause of Irish nationalism and independence, and like all the other remarkable Irish playwrights of his time, he was deeply involved in the national life of his country. Ireland was then excitingly alive, bubbling with political turbulence and remarkable creativeness. This was her supreme moment of political and artistic maturity, and the coincidence of these two aspects of spiritual effervescence which is and continues to be quite a landmark in the history of the world, testifies to the oneness of spirit and to its shaping force in history. Yeats's best plays are rooted in a reality which is profoundly human, and which in most cases also embraces Ireland; yet, neither the love of his country, nor the desire to contribute to the battle for her independence could turn his lofty genius away from his dedicated task of writing the poetry and the drama in which he believed, into trying to be the poet or playwright of the common man. He was, no doubt, haunted by the thought that some plays of his "might have sent out certain men the English shot", but he never wanted to write for the millions; he "wanted an unpopular theatre" because that was the theatre in which he believed. He did not want to fill vast halls; a drawing-room was enough for the creative audience which he had in mind. Contrary to the plight of most lyrical poets who cannot write dramatic poetry, Yeats was a born, histrionic performer and he had a great gift for self-dramatisation at the personal as well as the social level. The division between lyrical poetry and dramatic poetry is always artificial, for a dramatist always writes out of himself, and lyricism necessarily implies self-dramatisation. As Yeats said, "a poet makes poetry out of his conflicts", and what can be more heart-rendingly personal, more honestly displayed, and at the same time more self-dramatic and more arrestingly stated than:

> You think it horrible that lust and rage
> Should dance attendance upon my old age;
> They were not such a plague when I was young,
> What else have I to spur me into song?

or:

> I must lie down where all the ladders start
> In the foul rag and bone shop of the heart.

Yeats was a great poet and a genuine dramatist, and his plays' lack of popular success is due to his unwillingness to compromise, rather than to their dramatic failure. T. S. Eliot, who is well aware of Yeats's achievement in the theatre has summed it up with the words: "With the verse-play, on the other hand, the situation is reversed, because Yeats had nothing, and we had Yeats. He started writing plays at a time when the prose-play of contemporary life seemed triumphant, with an infinite future stretching before it; when the comedy of light farce dealt only with certain privileged strata of metropolitan life; and when the serious play tended to be an ephemeral tract on some transient social problem. We can begin to see now that even the imperfect early attempts he made are probably more permanent literature than the plays of Shaw; and that his dramatic work as a whole may prove a stronger defence against the successful urban Shaftesbury Avenue vulgarity which he opposed as stoutly as they."

Yeats's contemporaries, whether they wrote in verse or in prose, used myths, legends or historical subjects as means to move away from naturalism, followed in the wake of the great Romantics, whether they were English, French or German, and took as a model Shakespeare. None of them could free himself from his great shadow and from the echoes of the speech-forms which he had used. T. S. Eliot saw that this was as much a dead end for drama as Georgian poetry was a dead end for modern poetic sensibility. He realised that heroes and heroic life had retreated into the dark, and that his was the era of the common man who expressed his jumbled up emotions and his fragmented apprehensions of reality in racy, colloquial, syncopated, associational types of speech, as he himself had done in *The Waste Land* or in *Sweeney Agonistes*. He became convinced, and the notion is quite reasonable for a poet, that the main failure of late nineteenth and early twentieth century verse dramatists was a linguistic failure. They had sought to use a form of historical verse which, deprived of substance, sounded hollow and artificial, and they had dealt with themes which had no impact on modern sensibility. Ibsen had solved the problem by repudiating verse and Eliot felt that both he and Chekov had restricted their dramatic range by using prose instead of verse. "There are great prose dramatists—such as Ibsen and Chekov—who have at times done things of which I would not otherwise have supposed prose to be capable, but who seem to me, in spite of their success, to have been hampered in expression by writing in prose. This peculiar range of sensibility can be expressed by dramatic poetry, at its moments of greatest intensity. At such moments, we touch the border of those feelings which only music can express. We can never emulate music, because to arrive at the condition of music would be the annihilation of poetry, and especially of dramatic poetry. Nevertheless, I have before my eyes a kind of mirage of the perfection of verse drama, which would be a design of human action and of words, such as to present at once the two aspects of dramatic and of musical order."

We are back to Wagner and his notion that there is a fringe of feelings and meanings which cannot be caught in the web of words and which can only be suggested through music or through poetry analogical to music. This is of course a widely accepted assumption; still, the main problem consists in deciding what one means by poetry or by a poem. Can a drama be equated with a poem, and be something which, as Yeats tried to show, yields its wisdom, not through the time sequence of plot and character, but through its complex structures and through histrionic performance? Does poetry require a sustained metrical pattern? This is a much debated question, and it is not worth pursuing it at this moment, although one might state in passing that a poem, which is an organic whole, ought to have a sustained metrical rhythm which is part of the incantatory effect necessary to orientate and to stimulate the creative imagination of the reader or listener.

Eliot avoids this issue, which indeed does not require to be settled, by simply and rightly remarking that prose on the stage is as artificial as verse, and that verse can be as natural as prose. Having said that, he makes it clear that he believes that "the poetry of a great verse drama is not merely a decoration of a dialogue of a drama which could, as drama, be as well put in prose". He believes, on the contrary, that "it makes the drama itself different and more dramatic", and that verse, as a dramatic medium, is superior to prose: "To work out a play in verse is to be working like a musician as well as like a prose dramatist; . . . the verse dramatist must operate on you on two levels at once, dramatically with the character and plot . . . [and] underneath the action which should be perfectly intelligible, there should be a musical pattern which intensifies our excitement by reinforcing it with feelings from a deeper and less articulate level. Everybody knows that there are things that can be said in music that cannot be said in speech, and things that can be said in poetic drama that cannot be said in speech." Verse was therefore, according to Eliot a prerequisite of poetic drama, and it had to be a type of verse which would avoid the echo of Shakespeare, for; "I was persuaded", said Eliot, "that the primary failure of nineteenth-century poets when they wrote for the theatre (and most of the greatest English poets had tried their hand at drama) was not in their theatrical technique, but in their dramatic language; and that this was due largely to their limitation to a strict blank verse which, after extensive use for non-dramatic poetry, had lost the flexibility which blank verse must have if it is to give the effect of conversation. The rhythm of regular blank verse had become too remote from the movement of modern speech. Therefore what I kept in mind was the versification of *Everyman*, hoping that anything unusual in the sound of it would be, on the whole, advantageous." The point is clear; Eliot's main aim was to avoid the use of a verse which was part of the "high style" and of heroic drama which he did not wish to write. His task was Wordsworthian—a return to everyday speech, a shearing off of the decorative, pictorial and static elements, which, whether eighteenth century or Georgian, had, at their worst, turned poetry into a kind of refined product remote from life and which men could only indulge in when they were dressed in their Sunday best.

The need to harmonise dramatic verse with common language is of course practically as old as tragedy itself, and Aristotle had already noted that "in the theatre one has to use a type of verse which sounds least like verse, which mingles more easily than the others with common speech". Eliot has tried to base his rhythms upon common speech and to evolve a form of verse which can command all the resources of language. It is basically a flexible verse with three primary stresses, a caesura, possible secondary stresses and a varying number of syllables. It is a loose three-stressed line which has obviously benefited from Hopkins's theories about sprung rhythm, and which leaves plenty of scope for rhetoric and for variations according to the effective weight which it is made to carry. It can be tightened up and given the taut muscularity required to carry emotions by restricting the secondary stress and the number of syllables, or it can be loosened up and made to sidle along with prose when there is no intensity to convey. It is above all a functional line, Racinian in its transparency and avoidance of unnecessary images and metaphors. It is a line highly suitable for the themes in which speech must be based on everyday, living speech, and in his later plays it seems to have reached the same stage as the Alexandrine in which the rhetorical stress is more important than the strictly metrical stress.

Eliot has shown very early in his career that he was greatly concerned with the possibility of restoring poetic drama to the stage. By 1924, he had already stated that he wanted to write a drama of modern life in rhythmic prose. In fact, his vocation as a dramatist is part of his vocation as a poet, and he certainly did not turn to drama because he had exhausted his lyrical vein. Besides that, lyrical poetry itself is always dramatic in the sense that it underlies the separation of the singer from the state of things as they are, as they have been or as they might be, and Eliot's genius embraces meditative and humorous poetry as well as orthodox dramatic poetry. He is also endowed with an intellect and a range of philosophical knowledge rather rare among poets, and he possesses, in a large measure, the qualities of self-dramatisation, self-irony, psychological insight and imaginative empathy which are necessary to the dramatist. His earlier poems like *Prufrock* already show these qualities at work. His first truly dramatic attempt, *Sweeney Agonistes*, is a remarkable blend of modern verse and characterisation and has been a source of inspiration and imitation ever since its creation. Here we find the main iterations of speech of people of low intellect:

> Dusty: You've got to know what you want to ask them.
> Doris: You've got to know what you want to know.
> Dusty: It's no use asking them too much.
> Doris: It's no use asking them more than once.

and the notion that people can't communicate with one another, dear to Ionesco and Pinter. Here are also the snatches of jazz songs and the picture of boredom and emptiness which are so much part of our age. There is even the notion that "Any man might do a girl in, any man has to, needs to, wants to," which is an anticipation of Harry Monchensey's obsession, and of Celia Coppleston's fate. Eliot's aim was to reinstate poetic drama on the stage, and in order to do that: "poetic drama must enter into overt competition with prose drama. As I have said, people are prepared to put up with verse from the lips of personages dressed in the fashion of some distant age; they should be made to hear it from people dressed like ourselves, living in houses and apartments like ours, and using telephones and motor cars and radio sets. Audiences are prepared to accept poetry recited by a chorus, for that is a kind of poetry recital, which it does them credit to enjoy. And audiences (those who go to a verse play because it is in verse) expect poetry to be in rhythms which have lost touch with colloquial speech. What we have to do is to bring poetry into the world in which the audience lives and to which it returns when it leaves the theatre; not to transport the audience into some imaginary world totally unlike its own, an unreal world in which poetry is tolerated."

Eliot is an extremely conscious artist who knows what he wants to do, and who has the genius and the patience to pursue his aim to what he considers a satisfactory end. His aim was to win for poetic drama the place which it no longer held with the average theatre public. He has obviously not succeeded in holding the place which he had won, since poetic drama is at this moment out of favour. Neither has he been the only one responsible for whatever success poetic drama has had. Still, it can be conceded that he alone has achieved three things! He is the only one to have successfully established the use of verse in non-heroic, non-historical, everyday, comic or serious situations; he is the only one to have solved the problem of secular religious drama; and finally he is the one who has shown the greatest subtlety in using Greek myths as structures for the exploration of modern themes. He has not attempted, like Giraudoux or Anouilh, to modernise myths, through the use of topical language, situations and characters, and neither has he been heavy-handed and laboriously Freudian in the style of O'Neill in *Mourning becomes Electra*. He has dealt with Greek mythology by going back to its roots and by avoiding both ostentation and flippancy, and in so doing, he has treated it in a thoroughly adult way. What he has done is to weave modern, everyday situations into the framework of an ancient myth and then to winnow and to deepen these situations down to the point where, through the transparency of the naturalistic surface, shines the immanent, perennial reality of affective truths which are valid for all men at all time. Being a religious writer in the sense that he is constantly concerned with the interplay of immanence and transcendence, whether he disguises his pursuits under secular terminologies and analogies or uses straightforward Christian symbolism and references, Eliot is always in search of the kind of truth which relates his dramatic characters to the society to which they belong, and, beyond that, to a God-made creation.

He has used Greek myths in his last four plays, and in some instances he has so well covered up his tracks that, had he not had the honesty to declare his debt to the Greek dramatists, probably no one would have discovered it. Whether it is a comedy like *The Confidential Clerk* or serious dramas which, though they end with death, as in the case of the *Cocktail Party*, are no more serious than this comedy, the naturalistic surface of the situations and of the characters always casts out long shadows which plunge deep down into the perenniality of human life. Eliot is in this respect both Ibsenian and Strindbergian. His "naturalism" is a complex structure of essential traits and elements which act as a façade to hold the attention of the audience which, more often than not, finds itself unexpectedly out of its depth, and which once it has regained the shore spends its time trying to discover, with the help of very ingenious critics, how the magician has managed to lure it away towards the open sea and the depths, where it caught a frightening glimpse of the hidden reality which is a reflection of "le Dieu caché".

There are those who think that there has been a falling off of poetry after *Murder in the Cathedral*, and that Eliot, in trying to bring poetry to the stage has, in fact, arrived empty-handed on it and has, therefore made a fruitless journey. This is not so; for such a judgment presupposes, on the one hand, a lack of conscious planning and intention, and on the other, a desire to bring back to the stage a caparisoned, highly plumed muse whom everybody would recognise at once. This has never been Eliot's aim. In his lecture on Yeats, delivered in 1940, he said: "But another, and important cause of improvement is the gradual purging out of poetic ornament. This, perhaps, is the most painful part of labour, so far as the versification goes, of the modern poet who tries to write a play in verse. The course of improvement is towards greater and greater starkness. The beautiful line for its own sake is a luxury dangerous even for the poet who has made himself a virtuoso of the technique of the theatre. What is necessary is a beauty which shall not be in the line or in the isolable passage but woven into the dramatic texture itself; so that you can hardly say whether the lines give grandeur to the drama or whether it is the drama which turns the words into poetry." Donne's poetry rests on the texture of whole stanzas or a whole poem unfolding all the complexities of a thought or an emotion, and not on isolated lines. The symbolists had reacted vigorously against the tendency towards the jewelled line of the Parnassians and had insisted on the value of the poem as a unit. Eliot obviously held similar views, and he had already proved with *Sweeney Agonistes* and *The Rock* that he could write verse of unsurpassed flexibility and dramatic excellence. Still, these were only fragments and not full plays; it is therefore natural that he should have chosen to make his entry on the stage with a theme which offered as great a scope as possible to his already well-tried poetic gifts.

Being extremely clear-sighted about his aims and about the conception of his work, he has carefully explained in *Poetry and Drama* what he tried to do, what he thought he had achieved and what he thought he had failed to do. It would therefore be both unrewarding and out of place to labour his fully adequate expositions or to walk flat-footedly across his subtle analytical patterns. It should be sufficient to say that after *Murder in the Cathedral*, he was fully aware that, although he had certainly achieved something in taking his first steps in poetic drama, he had done so with the help of so many props and the use of so many already well-practised movements, that this merely proved that he could walk the path of poetic drama which, for the moment, had led him nowhere. This is not the place to analyse and to evaluate the overall aesthetic worth of *Murder in the Cathedral*. This has already been done so many times, that one could only contribute a little more assent or dissent to what has already been said. The specific concern of this study is with Eliot's original contribution to modern drama, under the three headings previously underlined. Still, lest one might think that *Murder in the Cathedral* is looked upon, either as Eliot's lonely achievement in the theatre, or, on the contrary, as some critics have suggested, as a dramatic attempt of scant interest, it ought perhaps to be stated that this play has plenty of sound claims to be looked upon as one of the best Christian plays of our time and as one of the rare and most valuable modern attempts at Christian tragedy. The action is neither carried out by the main character, nor does it grow linearly in time; it is a cumulative form of action, or should one rather say—a progressive dawning of light or illumination which enforces upon Becket the significance and necessity of his death, and upon the audience the moving wisdom that truth and the unfolding of the historical process cannot take place without the dire exaction of blood and tears. These are views prompted by the contemplation of the play as an intrinsic entity and which therefore do not allow the dramatic weaknesses, most of them detected by the author himself, to substantially detract from the high level of achievement. One has only to compare it with the other Beckets by Tennyson, Anouilh or Fry to realise that if Eliot cannot match Anouilh's dramatic skill, which is not needed in this case, the emotions with which he deals, have a true Aristotelian nobility and purity, and the martyred figure of his archbishop is likely to keep all the other attempts at depicting him, in the shade for a long time to come. Having said this, one ought also to say that if one examines *Murder in the Cathedral*, which is a great play, within the context of Eliot's dramatic *œuvre* intent in expressing both the great themes and preoccupations which haunt him, and above all, within his project of restoring verse to the stage, one is bound to confess that it is neither technically as successful nor as perfectly an integrated complex as *The Cocktail Party* or *The Confidential Clerk*.

The verse of *Murder in the Cathedral* remains somehow a motley garb which has not been fully woven into a single texture. The chorus's presence naturally slows down the action which, of course, is not the same type of action as that of the *Family Reunion*. There is here no dramatic suspense;

the audience knows what will come next, in the same way as Greek audiences knew every move of the great plays which they witnessed. In a sense, *Murder in the Cathedral* is a ritual; it is the re-enactment of a redeeming death; yet this does not fully dispose of the fact that a certain amount of the verse is either mono-voiced or static and that it acts as a kind of commentary to the action. The audiences know very clearly that they are listening to verse and generally they like it, for the audiences which love religious plays are special audiences conditioned to ritual, hieratic speech and noble elevation of style. But Eliot, who was intent in writing for as wide an audience as possible, knew that this was only a beginning. What he wanted was an audience who would neither look upon poetry as something unnatural, nor feel that it had to put on its special poetic soul whenever it was going to listen to a poetic play. Verse had therefore to be made as natural as possible, and transition between verse and prose or between different types of verse had to be avoided as being bewildering and as preventing the audience from giving itself un-selfconsciously to the flow of the dramatic action. "We should aim at a kind of verse in which everything can be said that has to be said; and when we find some situation which is intractable in verse, it is merely that our form of verse is inelastic. And if there prove to be scenes which we cannot put in verse, we must either develop our verse, or avoid having to introduce such scenes. For we have to accustom our audiences to verse to the point at which they will cease to be conscious of it; and to introduce prose dialogue, would only be to distract their attention from the play itself to the medium of its expression. But if our verse is to have so wide a range that it can say anything that has to be said, it follows that it will not be 'poetry' all the time. It will ony be 'poetry' when the dramatic situation has reached such a point of intensity that poetry becomes the natural utterance, because then it is the only language in which the emotions can be expressed at all."

For his next play, Eliot was determined to choose a contemporary theme and to evolve a form of verse close to contemporary speech. The result was *The Family Reunion*. The basic or the essential search was not very different from that of *Murder in the Cathedral*. It was the search for purity and holiness, and it is a search which will be continued in various forms in *The Cocktail Party* and in the plays which followed. It is in fact man's most fundamental search, his search for the essential truth which will enable him to close his eyes with the words *"in la sua volontade e nostra pace"*, and let his soul be enfolded in the great heart which he longs for. The prop of the historical subject having been discarded, Eliot replaced it by the prop of a Greek myth which, from now on, will be the infra-structure of his themes which are both modern and perennial. That of *The Family Reunion* comes from the *Oresteia* and more particularly from the *Choephori* and the *Eumenides*. Harry is a kind of Orestes who, instead of having killed his mother, may have killed his wife; at any rate he has the feeling that he may have done so.

Why? Well, as Sweeney in *Sweeney Agonistes* said "any man may do a girl in, any man wants to . . . "; besides, his father had certainly wanted to kill his mother, and Harry carries with him the guilt of his ancestry. He is therefore anything but the plain scion of a well-to-do family; he is a symbolic character, a kind of Hamlet at odds with his world. He is everyman in search of purity. He could be cured by psycho-analysis or by faith. The aunts and uncles are also at least as ambivalent as he is; they are what they are, and they are, at the same time, the commenting chorus. They are also the Erynnies who have to be turned by penance and acceptance of guilt, into the Eumenides; and, as such, they have given endless trouble to their author and to various producers who have directed the play. Then, there is the chauffeur, the police inspector and Harry's simpleton of a brother; we have altogether a naturalistic setting, a veneer of naturalism for the characters, and we have everywhere the lurking shadows of a symbolic world which carries the action deep down into the past and far and wide, beyond the social context to which these characters belong. This is an extremely subtle use of mythical and referential terms in order to lift the action out of the present and out of naturalism, into the world of imagination and poetry. It is obviously a big stride in the direction which Eliot had set himself; still, in spite of that, he was not yet fully out on the open road, on his own. Somehow, he was still trailed by the presence of the Eumenides, by the chorus which was seriously hampered by its ambivalent origin, and by flights of trance-like poetry through the medium of two stressed lines which fully blend neither with the choral verse nor with the dialogue. One could also note that the dramatic flow of the play had passed by the shores of Eliot's lyrical poetry, and had carried away a certain amount of material with it. This, of course, is unavoidable, and *The Cocktail Party*, which followed, carries with it scents and fragments from the same shores, something which emphasises, in fact, the consistency of Eliot's genius.

The Cocktail Party marks a definite progress in all the aspects of the drama which Eliot is trying to bring to life. The dramatic skill has increased, the blend between Greek myth and modern situation has been perfected, the verse has been fully integrated. It hardly carries any traces of choral speech; it still carries, when required, and it does so often enough, a good deal of ringing, very moving poetry. It has become, by now, a perfectly fluid and sinewy mode of expression. The different voices are clearly differentiated and the verse moves from very prosaic statements to rich poetry without faltering or attracting conscious attention to the transitions. The purple patches, the moments of lyricism disconnected from drama, have been firmly eliminated, and one has now a fluent, accurate and perfectly confident dramatic medium.

It seems clear that at this point Eliot has reached his aim and is now in control of the machine which he wishes to use. He has also succeeded in absorbing and integrating in his modern theme all the elements which he borrowed from the *Alcestis* of Euripides, and this time the integration is so complete, the permutations so subtle that one needs to be told in order to become fully aware of what they are. It is not necessary to unfold at length the intricacy of the two interwoven patterns; it will be sufficient to note the essential points. In Euripides

Alcestis consents to die in order to save her husband's life and Hercules, who is always in search of a good deed, decides to bring her back from the underworld. Alcestis corresponds to both Lavinia and Celia, that is to say to two aspects of femininity and to two levels of life in general. Lavinia does not die to save her husband; she merely leaves him alone so that he may find himself. When they both meet again after their brief respective journeys, not through the desert, but through life, they have both learnt to avoid excessive expectations; they both know now that they do not understand each other and that they must make the best of their humdrum existences. Celia is the woman who sacrifices herself. She began like Lavinia, Edward and Peter Quilpe by living in the dark, in a world of blindness or partial blindness from which they all have to move towards a form of light. But once Celia has been touched by grace and has achieved a vision of the true life, she can no longer accept compromise and humdrum existence, and she becomes a preordained martyr. Reilly is both Hercules and Pheres; he is the quizzical, jolly fellow, full of drink and songs, and he is the rescuer and healer who moves in an atmosphere of mystery which grips the play from the very moment the cocktail party of the beginning draws to a close and Edward remains alone with the strange, uninvited guest who seems no ordinary man.

The listener clutches in vain at the naturalistic setting and at the elements which first met his attention; he cannot help becoming more and more unsettled and more and more aware that things are anything but what they seem to be, and that he is moving in an ambivalent world, which is liable to confront him at any moment with profound and disturbing revelations. He soon discovers that the light-headed, Mayfair socialite, Julia, who talks like seven and seems such an inconsequential woman, is in fact the leader of the movement around her. She is endowed with strange powers which go further than Reilly's, and together with Alex, who seems at the beginning to be simply a gay dog about town, they are the "guardians", those who know and can guide others towards their salvation, either through humdrum existence, or, for those who are called, through martyrdom. Although the death of Celia could have been less colourful, and therefore more attuned to the tone and climate of the play, the religious theme emerges steadily and ripples out, embracing all the aspects of social life to which the characters belong, and carrying with it an aura of greater and greater light.

The next play, *The Confidential Clerk*, marks the completion of Eliot's search for a perfect blend of dramatic form with characters and action. The title itself—the "confidential clerk" and not the "private secretary"—is a way of distancing the play from naturalism and from the present. He has gone to Euripides, to *Ion* for the infra-structure of the action. The two worlds which are part of Eliot's thought are, this time, much better blended than in any other of his plays since they are close enough to form, at times, one, and since the play is primarily a comedy with very serious undertones and considerations. The two worlds are the world of commerce and the world of art. Art is more accessible than religion, and though it has had its monks and its martyrs, it neither requires the asceticism and sacrifices of religion, nor can it offer the same type of beatitude. So, Colby, who corresponds to Celia, will not die at the end of the play, but having discovered his true origins, and therefore having reached the stage of knowing himself, he will practise the art which he loves, and he may even enter religion, for he is a highly religious man. Before the final discovery of his vocation, music was for him a kind of religion, in the same way as ceramics and spiritualism were the private religions of Sir Claude and his wife. But there are no substitutes for religion, and those who lack faith or who try to replace it by something else can only lead fragmented existences which have no centre. Colby and the Mulhammers have their private gardens which they enter every now and then, but only Eggerson, who is a religious man, lives in an integrated world in which his garden is fruitful and is truly part of his life. Sir Claude and Colby realise that they lack the creative gift that they have longed for or thought they had, and, having discovered the truth about their origins and about their parents, they come to terms with life and decide each to follow the path which is marked for him. Sir Claude follows Edward Chamberlayne and finds a tolerable relationship with his wife; Colby renounces commerce, but not the world, to become an organist; and Eggerson, who has been a kind of guardian, like Julia and Alex, lets it be known that Colby might, in the end, take holy orders and work for his heavenly father. The tension of the play is lower than that of the *Cocktail*, but the blend of the various planes is more successful and the level more sustained. The verse has been pruned, chastened still more, and it offers no opportunity for elocution or elevated poetic diction. Even the most moving encounters between Colby and Sir Claude, and Colby and Lucasta, are so restrained, so controlled that the actors could not attempt to raise their voices and speak the lines as obvious verse without getting out of character.

Colby and Lucasta are not meant to be tempestuous, passionate or star-crossed lovers; they are everyday human beings, caught in the ice of situations where they struggle without shrieks or gestures, because that is not their nature; yet they are not less moving for that. They are no Cuchulain or Deirdre of the sorrows, and their subdued speech has the spare greyness of a world of cement and stones with, here and there, a patch of green. Of course most of what they say could have been said in prose, but who could have said it? Only Eliot himself, for no other dramatist has yet succeeded in blending such a sophisticated type of comedy with the religious seriousness which is part of his great gifts. Anouilh can be both comic and serious, but the two levels are never held together or projected through a highly sophisticated and, at the same time, deeply religious sensibility. The listener or reader is here given the facts, which the author has transmuted into an object which imposes its own terms. To refuse these terms, to say that *The Confidential Clerk* could have been written in prose or that it could have carried more poetry, is to ask for something very different from what the author tried to do or would have been willing to do. The kind of poetry which some poetry-lovers would wish to see on the stage cannot be associated with themes like that of *The Confidential Clerk* or the *The Elder Statesman*. It could only be associated with heroic or emotion-laden themes with highly individualised and partially symbolic characters which require another poet-playwright and, as far as one can see now, another public.

With *The Elder Statesman*, Eliot returns to a theme of guilt, akin to that of the *Family Reunion*. The difference is that here there has been no death, only two bad actions which weigh heavily on Lord Claverton's last days. He is an Ibsenian character, haunted by his past—alive in the shape of his ex-fellow student Gomez and his ex-sweetheart, Mrs. Carghill, who is related to Lady Mulhammer and, in certain respects, to Julia. Eliot has gone again to the Greeks for his scaffolding; this time he has made use of the *Oedipus Colonus* of Sophocles. Lord Claverton with Monica—Antigone, is on the way to the sacred grove where, purged of his guilt, he will die. His son Michael who has been caught in the web of his sense of guilt, is Polynices and also Harry of the *Family Reunion*. Lord Claverton needs no Tiresias to reveal to him the truth of his guilt; he knows it himself, he knows it perhaps with a rather disproportionate sense of its importance, for it is at all moments difficult to cast the same severity upon the minor failings of his youth. One could say that he is in need of self-mortification, but that only underscores his humanity and his humility. He is no prig, like his distant relation Harry Monchensy; he does not try to be a saint or to blame anyone for his failings; he only blames himself, even if he overstresses the blame. He is therefore very human; we look upon him as *"mon semblable, mon frère"*, leaving out the "hyprocrite", which he is not. He is too clear-sighted for that and too intent on his moral responsibilities, including those towards his son. He obviously would like to love and to be loved, and it is his love for his daughter which impels his confession and contrition. For the first time in Eliot's theatre, love between two young people comes to fruition and is presented as a normal manifestation of existence. The characterisation is even more marked than in any of the other plays, with the exception of Lord Claverton who is given extra-naturalistic dimensions which prepare the ground for his noble death; the other characters are, each with their respective traits, recognisably human. Gomez, Miss Campbell, Miss Piggot, the butler, are straight out of everyday life, and Charles and Monica close the play with the kind of moving love duet which neither Celia and Peter Quilpe, nor Colby and Lucasta had been able to sing. The play is bathed in an atmosphere of graceful mellowness, quaint wit and benignity which bespeaks of arrivals after tempests, and peace in quiet coves or sacred woods. Whatever the poet does after this play, he has certainly achieved the aims which he had set himself and he has produced a body of work which will earn him a high place among the dramatists of the world.

Eliot is not the only one to have striven to restore verse drama to the stage, there are quite a few poets who followed the same endeavours and not without success. In America the most important are A. MacLeish and Maxwell Anderson, who have a high reputation in their country and who have made valuable contributions to poetic drama. In this country the most important is of course Christopher Fry, who has enjoyed a good measure of commercial success with *The Lady is not for Burning, Venus Observed* and *The Dark is Light Enough*. Leaving out the intrinsic merit of Fry's plays, something which is not under examination in this work, the only point that matters here is his conception of poetry and the value of his verse; and on this score, it unfortunately seems to me that his achievement is rather limited. He obviously has a striking gift of words and glittering images and conceits, but he somehow seems to lack an innate sense of drama; therefore he is at his best in comedy of situations like the delightful and very successful *A Phoenix too Frequent* and in the only slightly less successful *The Lady is not for Burning*. When a certain amount of seriousness has to be carried by the theme, his sense of dramatic construction seems to let him down and one is left with something which does not quite cohere into a good play. One of the main reasons for this failure to deal adequately with serious subjects seems to be that for Fry, poetry is the opposite of prose. Far from trying to conceal it as Eliot tried to do, or to use it as a purely utilitarian instrument it becomes, on the contrary, poetry for poetry's sake and sometimes poetry as decoration and virtuosity. The result is that most of his characters talk alike, exhibiting the same verbal brilliance and trying to outshine one another in puns, conceits and verbal displays, so that, in the end, speech is less an expression of character than an explosion of verbal fireworks prompted by occasions and situations. The words seem to hover above the characters who do not evolve, and are like figures clad in glittering garbs, singularly lacking, at times, in emotions or human substance. This is of no importance in comedies of situation in which verbal wit and exuberance of language inevitably carry the play forward in a dazzle of words. In that domain, Fry is a master and he had only one rival, Dylan Thomas, who, had he lived, might have proved a major playwright. Dylan Thomas had, besides true poetic genius, a remarkable gift of characterisation through memorable images and word arrangements. Fry, in spite of his obvious love of men and his passionate defence of noble ideals, seems to me to be endowed with the kind of poetic mind which not only transmutes reality and is at its best when it operates at one remove from it, but also finds it difficult, perhaps because of extremely refined and over-shy sensibility, to be profoundly and directly committed to the affective life of his characters. Not unlike Shaw in this respect, he displays a certain headiness which both emphasises the cerebral at the expense of the affective and also allows the characters to loose themselves in the excitement of words. Even a serious play like *The First Born*, in which the dramatic action is ready made, does not quite rise beyond the level of good biblical pageantry in which the characters remain pinned to their own background. None of them quite succeeds in stepping out of a given time into timelessness. *A Sleep of Prisoners*, which is a moving meditation on the human predicament, on the page, does not quite crystallise into a dramatic action.

Fry has perhaps too much of the lyrical poet in himself and not enough of the dramatist. As full of humanity as any of our zealous and vocal contemporary reformers Fry, like the much

regretted John Whiting, cannot look upon the artist as a
political propagandist or a social reformer, he is therefore
ill at ease in the predominantly naturalistic and leftish
climate of the moment. He is obviously intent on conveying
essential things and on listening and reporting to those prepared to give him their attention, about what he has heard
and seen beyond the tumult and the distant horizon. Will he
succeed, and can he succeed in regaining a hearing? The
question, alas, is open to doubt at this moment, and in spite
of the best possible will towards his efforts and integrity of
purpose, his verse, which can glitter and sparkle like frost in
the moonlight, generally lacks a rhythmic pattern, something
which is not at all a matter of carefully controlled prosody but
of emotional ground swell. It is the ground rhythm of profound emotional involvement, imaginatively felt and
expressed and which one finds for instance in *Measure for
Measure* and *A Winter's Tale*, as well as in *Hamlet* or *Lear*.
Lacking in rhythm, Fry's verse shows, at times, no rhetorical
advantage by being read as verse instead of higly coloured
prose.

With Eliot, the rhythms are on the contrary clear-cut
and perfectly blended with the rhetorical requirements of the
meaning. Whatever the paucity of metaphors and images,
Eliot's rhythmical patterns are always recognisable and they
contribute to the orchestration of his plays and to the pervad-
ing influence of music in the artistic experience conveyed.
Curtmantle, Fry's last play, has been aptly described as a
noble failure, something which calls for admiration for the
effort, the aims and the achievement which is the high-water
mark of Fry's theatre. With this play, he has at last succeeded
in more or less disposing of the criticism that his language
was static and uniform, and his poetry a mere adornment to
themes which could have been dressed in a less gaudy apparel.
Fry's most successful plays, like *A Phoenix too Frequent*, *The
Lady is not for Burning*, *Venus Observed* and *The Dark is
Light Enough*, are above all vehicles for star performers who
have so completely absorbed the parts which they played that
one remembers them and practically nothing of the substance

which they so fully transmuted into their personalities. *The Dark is Light Enough* is above all the mellifluous, wide-ranging voice and mastery of Dame Edith Evans, who hovers over the play like a phoenix above its ashes. True, the play was written with her in mind; therefore, the fact that she becomes the whole play is in many ways a measure of Fry's talent and verbal dexterity; still in spite of great stylistic progress by comparison with the previous plays, and in spite of Dame Edith, the play's dramatic weaknesses remain unredeemable.

The same dramatic weakness weighs practically as heavily over *Curtmantle*, and has prevented Fry from making of it a good play. The play still carries a good deal of periphrastic circumnambulation, didacticism and rhetoric which could have been shed with advantage, but on the whole, the gratuitious images, antitheses and conceits which dogged the previous plays have been dropped, and the language is taut, sinewy, at times brilliantly epigrammatic and full of felicitous phrases and passages which aptly sum up situations and attitudes. Yet remarkable though the language is, it has not been diversified, at least, not enough, according to characters. This failing is part of the crucial weakness which is Fry's main problem once more illustrated by this play, and which is that he has been unable to transcend the inherent difficulties of his theme and the main failing of his dramatic talent. The handling of the theme may have been dictated partly by historical data and present circumstances, and partly by natural leanings and inclinations. Eliot having made of Becket the sole protagonist of his memorable play, it was, no doubt, difficult to bring Becket back to full pre-eminence on the stage. Anouilh has tried it, and whatever the failings of his play, he has locked Becket and the King in a deeply human and striking relationship which wrapped up their tortured quarrel into a type of poignancy and sorrow which cast its moving light over dramatic flaws and cannot but leave its imprint upon the memory. Fry has concentrated upon one single protagonist—the King, and Becket is merely a sparring partner. The conflict which opposes them is not a human conflict but a conflict or ideas, shorn of any human cries and tears which move the heart. The King is intent in giving laws to England. That is a noble aim, but it is not something dramatic. Although the King's name and presence ring from page to page, from scene to scene from the prologue to his unconscionably long last moments, the King does not quite come alive, and his isolation, defeat and death leave the spectator practically unmoved. Having made of the King the centre of the play, Fry tries to bring him to life, not directly, but by a series of tableaux and secondary little scenes which are historically accurate, but which not only fail to give body and soul to the main character, but disperse the dramatic interest, because of their diffuseness. Life can only be given from within, and not from without. Here we touch upon the central weakness of the play which is the dramatist's inability to create a truly living character and who therefore tries to palliate this weakness by creating atmosphere through peripheral characters and situations. The result is that the play, instead of developing in depth and in human texture and complexity, as the splendid first act suggests, sinks into prolixities and long-drawn-out historical details which cause the dramatic temperature to cool down so much that it can never again rise to the boil. The second act, with its court scenes and with the royal children's futile squabbles, is particularly lacking in dramatic tension which is difficult to maintain owing to the episodic nature of the play and the lack of real humanity in the characters. The attempt to unify the action and to liberate it from the trappings of space and time by making it look as if it were performed on the stage of memory is a rather clumsy and unsatisfactory device in a play of sequential pageantry. The final result is a fine piece of historical pageantry, well written, quite rich in memorable phrases and moments of illumination, but failing to cohere into a memorable play and experience, something which Fry has sought with such obvious painstaking honesty, integrity and pertinacity that one feels very sad at not being able to applaud him whole-heartedly.

Together with Fry, one must mention the left-wing poet-dramatists of the thirties—Auden and Spender, the religious poet-dramatists, Anne Ridler, Norman Nicholson and the successful Ronald Duncan.* Above all, one must not forget Dylan Thomas, the most original poetic talent since Eliot and whose only play, *Under Milkwood*, written in prose, shows that he had a remarkable sense of characterisation and drama and that his early death has cut short a promising dramatic career. No discussion on the place and importance of poetic drama of the post-war years could afford not to mention the name of E. Martin Browne, who has produced every one of T. S. Eliot's plays and has made a unique contribution to the development of poetic and religious drama in the commercial theatre and throughout the repertory movement.

* These poets' work is neither part of the period under study, nor part of the question under examination.

CHAPTER FIVE

DRAMA IN ENGLAND

THE revival of poetry and poetic drama which coincided with the emotional turbulence and excitement of the thirties and the forties, during the second world war and after, seemed by the 1950's to have expended its momentum. By that time the enthusiasm of the wartime collaboration between Russia and the West had given way to openly divergent aims and ambitions and to a stalemate in military strength, the import of which was becoming more and more terrifying. The world, divided into two increasingly antagonistic ideologies, was strewn with smouldering conflicts in Europe and the Middle East, and open warfare in Asia and Africa. Idealism was definitely at a low ebb and the masses of mankind torn between outbursts of facile optimism and lurking fears were neither able to appreciate nor truly interested in deeply stirring artistic experiences which shallow or frozen-up contemporary sensibility was unable to absorb. It looked as if the world, exhausted by the profound emotions and tragic moments it had lived through, was no longer able to feel deeply or to indulge in exalting hopes or violent despair. It was turning to a type of greyness and cynicism which could only be shaken up by shock treatment or sensationalism.

Television's ever widening range and the films were the adequate means through which the masses of the world could satisfy their craving for being entertained and titillated without any serious mental or affective contributions. There seemed to be no ground left for enthusiasm, passion or ideals in a world in which life looked uncertain, flimsy or futile. Whenever life does not seem to bear thinking, the mind can only be a source of terrors and the cult of sensationalism is the only pleasurable, anaesthetising occupation. Painting was moving towards greater abstraction and stylisation, or towards a gratuitous and surrealistic type of self-expression which is a form of sensualism. The experimental novel in France, although interesting as exploration, betrays nevertheless earthbound imagination and anaemic affectivity due to the fact that memory's cupboards are, like Mother Hubbard's, practically empty. On the other hand, the cinema new wave associated with this type of writing and now moving towards associationism, sensualism and simultaneity of past and present, away from post-war Italian verism, is still very much alive.

French and German drama had kept pace with the new climate of nihilism and despair; not so English drama which, in the early fifties, in the hey-day of the welfare state was still fully immersed in traditional middle-class or upper middle-class subjects, and in a fading interest for poetic drama, mostly based on religious themes, unable to meet the expectations of the increasingly politically conscious and dissatisfied middle class which was still the main supporter of the theatre. O'Casey, the immortal author of *Juno and the Paycock* and *The Plough and the Stars*, was continuing his brilliant career with those astounding blends of earthiness and wit, pathos and comedy which seem to me the privilege of the Irish. O'Casey, like Synge and Shaw, is a major dramatist whose reputation, like theirs and that of Yeats, belongs to the early part of this century and not to the fifties. The other leading prose-dramatists of the day like Priestley, Rattigan, Coward, Graham Greene, N. C. Hunter and Peter Ustinov were writing good, entertaining, well-constructed plays whose only fault was that they did not quite correspond to the mood of frustration and exacerbation which was that of the middle fifties. The plays which were truly exciting, and which showed that their authors had their fingers right on the pulse of the young generation, were the plays which were coming from the continent and which were occupying, at that time, a large share of the London stage. They were the plays of Sartre, Brecht, Hochwalder, Betti, Anouilh, Beckett and, slightly later, Ionesco. These plays were something more than entertainment; they all tried to come to grips with topical problems and through renewed dramaturgy and extended use of language, they had, on the whole, enlarged the scope of human experience. They were not only good theatre, they were theatre in the process of transformation and widening of range, and their presence on the English stage only served to emphasise what was already widely felt—the need for an experimental type of theatre fully attuned to contemporary life and dealing with problems and situations which were part and parcel of the psyche of a contemporary audience.

Some sections of the public were fully aware of this need, some writers were aware of it too, but nothing could have been done without the necessary organisations to look for the plays and to produce them, and there is no doubt that the success of the new drama, whatever its worth, is greatly due to the theatrical organisations which made this possible. First and foremost in this field stands the English Stage Company, with its founders—Lord Harewood, Neville Blond and the indefatigable Ronald Duncan, poet and dramatist of under-valued reputation. But the man who has borne the main responsibilities and made the success of the English Stage Company possible is undeniably George Devine, with the help of his assistant-director, Tony Richardson. They had been thinking about the planning and the running of a theatre like the Royal Court for years, and when success came at last in 1956, after having been sorely tested and tried, it was only their courage and pertinacity which had enabled them to go on working and to win the day.

John Osborne's famed play, *Look back in Anger,* which was launched on 8 May 1956 was anything but a success at the start. The critical reception was rather mixed and on the whole lukewarm. The weaknesses of this play were too clearly apparent to be missed. First of all it is not a well-constructed, coherent play; the first act is a long monologue with Cliff used as compère for Jimmy Porter's sallies and vituperations. Alison's forbearance and some of the actions of the play are contrived and ill accord with its naturalistic setting. The autobiographical element is too evident and it makes Jimmy

Porter's self-pity all the more unpalatable. The episode about the Spanish war is sentimental, and the end of the play is thoroughly melodramatic. The dialogue is brilliant, non-naturalistic, admirably stylised and full of memorable phrases which clothe Jimmy Porter in dramatic reality. One could dissociate oneself from the excessive rage, the lack of idealism and from Jimmy Porter's obsessions with futile objects of censure or redress, but one could not miss the authentic ring of truth in the frustration which he voices. The audiences did not miss it and they responded with alacrity to this raw, exacerbated sensibility and exuberance of language. Fry's word displays, unconnected with feelings, were often enough linguistic acrobatics which amused, and in some cases, delighted without ever bruising the most delicate skins; Jimmy Porter's invectives and cries of rage left no one unperturbed. One might approve or disapprove of them, but one could not slough them off or ignore them; they were too sharp and too real. Without feeling as much done down as he does, and as personally involved in the world's stupidity and disregard of human suffering and hopes, one cannot fail to aver that the reckless, cruel way in which human beings faced one another in Hungary, Suez and in other parts of the earth were anything but meant to nurse optimism and self-satisfaction in human hearts. Jimmy Porter was of course too loud-mouthed; yet his revolt and his attitude of protest were widely shared; his senseless cruelty, which was mostly self-flagellation, and his evident maladjustment were, if not approved, at least excused, and John Osborne was hailed as the mouthpiece of his generation. Jimmy Porterism was born and in no time, John Osborne was followed by Brendan Behan, Shellagh Delaney, Arnold Wesker, Willis Hall and John Arden who voiced in their works the same restlessness and the desperation of rootless individuals unhappy and at war with the social order, either without knowing why, or on the contrary, as in the case of Wesker, knowing only too well the kind of political and economic changes that they would like to make. Whether they are of working-class origins, educated through the welfare state, pure and simple down-and-outs or former lawbreakers, most of these writers' dramatic characters can only live on the fringe of society; their attitude is one of revolt, day-dreaming and pursuits of new worlds. If, on the whole, they are neither coherent nor explicit about the world they would like to bring about, they are very vocal about their itches and about their emotional bitterness which either wells up without apparent causes, or is on the contrary didactically laden with social protest, as is the case with Wesker. The setting of these cries of protest and the behaviour and language of the individuals involved are generally naturalistic, and in some cases to the point of parodying life. Osborne's naturalism is generally confined to the setting and to the topicalities which are parts of his social protest, while his characters are definitely actors and his language is too articulate and too stylised to be called naturalistic. Even *Look Back in Anger* which has been the signal of the revival of naturalism on the stage cannot be described as a naturalistic play.

Osborne's next play, *The Entertainer*, clearly shows the influence of Brecht with its mixture of music-hall numbers and realistic scenes of the life of Archie Rice—a decaying, corny, stale comedian who is obviously the epitome of the decaying society and entertainment world in which he lives. As he himself says, "he is dead behind the eyes and nothing matters", and with the exception of his father, Billie Rice, who represents the Edwardian age, which in this case becomes an object of nostalgia instead of an object of anger and invective as in the previous play, none of the characters is worthy of much sympathy. The main part was made very much alive by the virtuoso performance of Sir Lawrence Olivier; yet it is obvious that the root or the cause of Archie Rice's failures lies not in the world around him, but in himself. He is more or less on the same low level as the dull audiences he vainly caters for, and the heavy-handed social satire and the melodramatic use of the Suez affair are both contrived and completely unrewarding in the climate of unrelieved mediocrity and insensitiveness in which Archie lives; so that the curtain falls on an atmosphere of dull, uninspiring greyness. *The World of Paul Slickey* shows Osborne at his worst, and public and critics were utterly justified in refusing to be bludgeoned into accepting this concoction of crudities and boredom as musical social satire. The least said about it the better, for there is nothing to be said in its favour and it is very sad to see such a total failure. Flailing about like a man stung by wasps is no substitute for coherent entertainment, and Osborne going up in noise and smoke in all directions like a catherine wheel, won't contribute anything towards the rescue of the dying music hall. Osborne has obviously no gifts for light satire or for song-writing and the antics of *The World of Paul Slickey* would even bore an end-of-term school-children's party.

In spite of its success, greatly due to Albert Finney's masterly performance, *Luther*, which followed, did not succeed in dissipating the forebodings about Osborne's dramatic limitations. *Luther* is by no means a good play; it lacks dramatic cohesion and movement; it is a succession of tableaux which are not quite held together either by a real growth of character or by sustained dramatic action and conflict between the characters. On the other hand, the subject of *Luther* offered Osborne admirable possibilities which he has successfully seized in order to continue to vent his anger and to use his colourful language. This play makes it of course clear that he is fundamentally unable to deal with religion, except as a means of clowning and sensationalism, as is the case with the scene of the sale of indulgences, and with the scene with the Pope about to go hunting; still, he can easily avoid religious subjects. On the credit side, Osborne has shown that he can skilfully handle historical material and that he can make good use of documentary sources for the reconstruction of dialogue. If *Luther* is neither a great play nor quite a first-rate play, it is a reasonably good piece of dramatic craft and, all in all, quite a credit to its author. It shows that Osborne can use pre-existing material partly to infuse it with his own sensibility and with modern feelings, and partly to draw it towards contemporaneity so as to move from mere chronicle to good dramatic entertainment.

With *Plays for England* we are partly back to *The World of*

Paul Slickey, with the same kind of incompetence and similarly disastrous results. One can neither comprehend how a man of Osborne's talents can try to pass such a jumble of tedious half-baked notions as *The Blood of the Banbergs* as a play, nor how he can allow himself to offer them to the public as entertainment or social satire. The second play *Under Plain Cover,* although it starts well, with a series of Genet-like fantasies in the course of which a young couple indulge their love of dressing up and of playing parts so as to show their state of maladjustment and isolation from society, soon turns to melodramatic crudity with the appearance of Osborne's rankling obsession which is the press reporter who discovers them and reveals their uncertain relations to the world at large. After that, the play collapses in incoherence, boredom and infantile rhapsodising about knickers, something altogether so unbearable as to send any adult audience scurrying out of their seats.

Osborne's last play, *Inadmissible Evidence,* is a great improvement on his last two, and a convincing reassertion of his dramatic abilities. It shows clearly that when he is working on a theme which is within his range, he is capable of achieving considerable success. The theme is again anger and frustration. This time it is the anger and frustration of a kind of Willy Lowman of the Bar, called Bill Maitland, who can no longer cope with his marital and extra-marital problems and with the cares which his office imposes upon him. The play opens with a nightmare scene, in which the main character, remarkably portrayed by Nicol Williamson, displays the state of disintegration and panic to which his lies, lust, mediocrity and shallowness have brought him. At first, the motivation for this kind of situation is no more understandable than the much talked about drunkenness or the peccadillo which has supposedly put him on the wrong side of the law, but once real life begins, one can see how he disintegrates and why he can no longer cope with his crowding fears. The obverse of this telling demonstration is, of course, that his shiftiness, mediocrity, shallowness and mendacity are such as to render him unworthy of any deep sympathy or tragic compassion. It

8

is as difficult to imagine him as a proficient and honest solicitor as it is difficult to see him as attractive to women and capable of inspiring love. The final scene when he is confronted with his mistress is as unconvincing as the latter's exit. Still, it is as well to point out that psychological verisimilitude is neither the main aim of the play, nor Osborne's strong point.

Osborne has, like Bernard Shaw, a passionate intellect and he cares passionately about certain things which he wishes to put right. What matters for him is the urge to expose what he objects to and to uphold what he believes, through themes and characters which offer him the opportunity to do so. If, therefore, the characters of this play look rather weak and shadowy, the reason is that the main protagonist to which they are all related is more a mouthpiece for the author than a fully fledged dramatic character. Mrs. Garnsey, unfolding her tale of woes, is obviously echoing Bill Maitland's troubles in another key; still, the important point is that the latter is so obsessed by his failure and loss of control that he can hear no-one but himself; that is why all women's parts are played by the same actress and the homosexual is played by his assistant. The homosexual is the only one who moves him to action, perhaps in order to project his own self-pity.

The picture of the affluent society is excellent. The descriptions of the small car owners, of the teenagers and of the sex-war, are, in spite of the fact that the shadow of the author deprives them of a certain amount of dramatic force, well observed, vividly phrased and add to the comic elements of the play. Bill Maitland riddled with self-pity and self-guilt remains more socially circumscribed than Jimmy Porter or Willy Loman. He will only find echoes among the mediocre and the frustrated whose misplaced hopes have failed to materialise. He may draw condescending pity and sympathy but no tragic emotions and catharsis, but this does not prevent the play from being good theatre, assured of success.

Osborne is refreshingly free from notions of avant gardeism or technical novelty; yet he does not lack dramatic skill, in fact his skill is at times over-evident. But his strong point is language, language not so much language in dialogue form, as in alternating or interwoven soliloquies which carry the play forward through memorable moments of brilliant wit and striking invective. No one in the English theatre, with the exception of Arden, shows the same command of language.

Arnold Wesker is another member of the new wave of British dramatists who owes his reputation mostly to the steady support of the Royal Court. He has had a very swift rise (his first play was produced in July 1958) on a relatively small body of work which for the moment at least seems to be of rather limited scope. He is a very active, industrious writer dedicated to the task of bringing art and enlightenment to the masses. Although ideas and ideals do not necessarily make good art, his enthusiasm is infectious and he has quite a following. Even if one might doubt the soundness of his approach to the problem of enlightening the masses and of improving their lot through art, his heart is in the right place, and one cannot but admire and be prepared to applaud his zeal. Besides that, whatever he may lack, he does not lack boldness of conception; it may very well verge on the border of excessive self-confidence, but, up to a point, he has succeeded in justifying it. What other writer, except Wesker, would dare to talk about, let alone plan and produce in sequence, a trilogy! The very word itself is awe-inspiring, and to plan to write a panorama of working-class life through twenty years of the life of a family, and to have it produced in one of the leading theatres of the western world, is no mean achievement which says as much for Wesker's boldness and energy as for the courage of the Royal Court theatre. Few young writers, with the exception of John Arden, another Royal Court dramatist, have ever been given such unstinted support by a theatrical management. Whatever the final outcome, and whatever the value of the achievement, the effort is justified in the sense that it shows a devotion to art which can only be an inspiration for others.

It is, however, difficult to be really enthusiastic about Wesker's achievement. None of the three plays of the trilogy is truly a good play. They all share certain common faults, which are poor construction, over-stressed didacticism, incoherence and melodramatic touches, to say nothing of the crude naturalism which, in some cases, is carried to excessive, and therefore, unreal extremes. There is in every case too much propaganda and too much proselytising oratory. *Chicken Soup with Barley*, the first of the trilogy, deals with the life of the Kahns between 1936 and 1956, and the characters, under the plain cover of naturalism and verisimilitude, are used for the demonstration of social theories and points of view. The social plane swamps the personal plane; the distance between the historical events which seem to affect the lives of these individuals and the historical worth of these same individuals is too great to allow a truly integrated dramatic action. There has been no transmutation, and the impact of the Spanish war and of the Hungarian revolution upon the social life and character of the Kahns barely rises above the level of journalistic reportage or dramatised documentary. In spite of the praise lavished on *Roots*, a good deal no doubt due to the outstanding performance of Joan Plowright and to some good aspects of the play, the faulty, laboured construction and repetitiousness of the first two acts, together with the slanted naturalism, seem to make it difficult to call *Roots* a truly good play. The play, which is obviously autobiographical and didactic, makes of Ronnie a pedant and a bore that only a yokel could admire, and Beatie is no yokel. The notion of a so-called cleavage between town and country is at war with the naturalism of the play which is not quite transmuted by Beatie's dance or by her moving illumination at the end of the play. *I am Talking about Jerusalem*, a more ambitious play than the other two, deals with the failure of the experiment of Ada and Dave of the Kahn family, with a life of Morrisian devotion to craft and art in Norfolk. Dave loses his job through pilfering and after that, having failed to find a means of making a living in the country, they go back to town life, leaving the audience and themselves to wonder about the value of the experience that they have undergone.

The Kitchen, an early one-act play written in 1958, is the

best play of Wesker's, to date. If the naturalism is again faulty
in the sense that no kitchen could really work in the way this
kitchen works, Wesker has admirably caught the atmosphere
of a closed, cooped world, with tensions and passions exacerbated by the noise, the heat, the hurly-burly of work and the
general incomprehension; the final explosion of violence of
the German cook is credible, real and impressive. There have
been byzantine, recondite critics who have seen in this
kitchen a microcosm of the world. Good luck to them! One
would have thought that the very narrow and overworked
naturalism precluded such flights of fancy, though of course
it is true to say that this kitchen exteriorises many aspects of
human life, the most important being the frustration and
hopelessness of certain lives in circumscribed horizons.

Chips with Everything is a *pièce à thèse* about class war which
is as fustian as the age of crinolines. The squares and circles
are carefully laid out at the beginning, the ground clearly
mapped out and the audience soon knows what will happen
and which side will win, so it can give itself wholeheartedly
to the perennial enjoyment of square-bashing and barrack life
in the tradition of *Le train de 8ʰ 47* or *Worm's Eye View.*
The characterisation of the recruits and officers is pretty
mechanical and on the whole pertaining more to farce than to
psychological drama. The officers are, as expected, thoroughly
incompetent, and only barely manage to keep the proles in
chains through the reflexes of their class which is used to
crushing rebellion through apathy and polite indifference.
This point is certainly well observed; so it the usual ambivalent attitude of the non-commissioned officers who bully the
men on the parade ground and find themselves completely at
one with them off duty. Pip is too obviously destined to have
pips on his shoulders; his discovery of working-class life, his
attempts to switch the concert performance from jazz music
to folksy art, together with his obviously author-directed turns
about, are unfortunately unconvincing. The naturalism of
the parade ground is caricatural, and Nigel Dennis, in
Encounter of August 1962, gave a rather apt description of
it: "*Chips with Everything,* to put it as simply as possible, is a

direct reproduction upon a stage of military training as it actually is. It requires a stage only because it requires an audience, and an audience must be seated and housed. That is why *Chips with Everything* is at the Vaudeville Theatre and not at Aldershot. In putting it across, Sergeant-Major Brittain laboured under difficulties that would have crushed a playwright. . . . Brittain had nothing to follow but the official Manual of Drill—and this, we suspect, is the only reason why so many people think that *Chips with Everything* is a play. For the modern fashion in playwriting is one of direct instruction rather than imaginative appeal, and there could be no better model for this manner than a Forces' handbook. . . . The marvel of *Chips with Everything*—would not *Chips on Everyone* have indicated better what Brittain was up against?—is that it succeeds in saying all these important things without ever becoming in the least degree fanciful and intellectual: we can think of no other documentary in which the *simple* truth carries anything like the same burden. . . . Brittain, as we have said before, did not set out to write a play, nor has he, in fact, done so. But one feels that he came within an ace of trying, and that his resistance to the temptation is precisely the measure of his success." Still, it is obvious that Wesker has dramatic talents, and once he has shed his urge to preach, to convert or overtly to expose, he will allow his skill at characterisation to find its true place in his drama.

Another playwright who has been given great support by the Royal Court Theatre and who, for the moment, has not achieved the full measure of his success is John Arden. His *Live Like Pigs* is merely part and parcel of the very undistinguished contemporary wave of naturalism. His *Sergeant Musgrave's Dance*, a striking play and one of the best plays of the last ten years, is a very different matter. Although Arden lacks the technical skill and lyrical gift of Brecht whom he at times imitates, he nevertheless shows qualities of originality, vision and poetic language which make of him a dramatist of real promise. He is obviously still finding his way, but on the strength of *Sergeant Musgrave's Dance*, it is safe to say that he shows greater possibilities of originality than most of his contemporaries.

The case of Harold Pinter is the most fascinating of the English theatre at this moment. Some critics think that far more than the fantastical verse plays of Fry or the verse-in-disguise plays of Eliot, Pinter's works are the true poetic drama of our time and that in the long run he is likely to turn out the greatest of them all. Another critic says that the junk and clutter of *The Caretaker* is pure Ionesco and that so is the failure of communication, the desperate search for what can never be achieved, the disintegration of language and the disintegration of psychology. To yet another, Pinter is the perfect dramatist of the absurd, whatever this high-sounding, awe-inspiring label may mean. Another critic's reaction after seeing *The Caretaker* was a storm of tears. Without my going as far as shedding tears, this play, which was widely acclaimed and highly praised by many critics, left me rather un-enthusiastic, although it persuaded me of one very important thing, which is that Pinter is, among other things, a most skilful craftsman. He can construct plays like jigsaw puzzles and he can fuse together Eliot's, Ionesco's and Beckett's rhythms into structures which look deceptively naturalistic, but are in fact contrived, and sometimes, of course, much too much so. His tramps, which are closely connected with Beckett's world, are the acme of tramphood; they look so natural as to be quite unnatural; they are rigged up for what obviously looks like a performance, and they go through the tricks of vagrancy and doss-life in a way which can become distinctly caricatural by being overladen with properties which had already been put to a more organic use by Beckett or by Charlie Chaplin. At least such was the case in the pro-duction which I saw. Shoes and hats are much tossed about, and their language oscillates between mechanical iterations in the Ionesco manner, poetic passages or statements com-pletely unconnected with the situation in which they find themselves and which are used so as to show that they are confronted with mysteries which they cannot solve and ten-sions which numb their minds and only enable them to use language as a disguise, and not as a means of communication.

This process which Eliot had explored in *Sweeney Agonistes* is here effectively used in moments when an emotion-laden climate counterpoints the inanity of speech. There is, of course a world of difference between Beckett's tramps and Pinter's tramps. Beckett's tramps are classless tramps and they are above all two men, two samples of humankind waiting for the allaying of a fear and the satisfaction of a longing as old as man. They needed not be tramps, they are two archetypal men, two universal individuals. Pinter's tramps belong to a definite social background and therefore lack universality. Above all, there is a world of difference between waiting for Godot and waiting to go to Sidcup, which looks somewhat like a device in order to contrive mystery. *Waiting for Godot* is a static play and its staticity is inherent to the theme; the two tramps wait for Godot who is worth waiting for. Pinter's play is mainly static by contrivance, and a great deal of the mythology weaved by benevolent critics round the comings and goings of the three characters seems to me intellectual gymnastics, excellent for those who practise it, but pretty useless for anyone who has not been completely struck by this magic or cannot fully comply with this kind of let-us-pretend game. It takes more than these over-simplified ingredients to make myth. One cannot universalise upon the bare fact that Davies claims to have lost his identity because he can neither find a proper pair of shoes nor tame the weather, so that he may go to Sidcup. Neither can one seriously talk about Davies's tragic fate as being similar to that of Adam unparadised and equate his petty egoism, the egoism of an altogether futile little man, with hubris—the sin of mankind. To inflate this skilfully contrived piece of naturalism into talks of universality and tragedy is merely to turn Sidcup into a new Jerusalem and to impose upon the play a burden which the text itself does not claim, and which the author's modesty and integrity does not imply. The inflation lies more in the production and in the critical eulogies than in the text itself. The textual centre of gravity of the play is the subtle and moving personal relationship between

the two brothers. This relationship is disturbed by the tramp
who, in the London production, reached caricatural proportions and was surrounded by a kind of shallow symbolism
which considerably dispelled the real simplicity of the play
and the genuine, moving plight of the mentally disturbed
brother.

One knows only too well that everything has already been
said and that there is little room left for originality. Therefore Pinter's originality lies above all in his skilful use of
attitudes, situations and notions which have already had quite
a run; yet, this is not in the least derogatory. Neither Shakespeare nor Racine invented much of the basic material which
they used. One would think that anyone familiar with Maeterlinck's plays would be familiar with the notion of the impossibility of communicating one's profound, intimate feelings
and with that of the crowding mystery and tension which can
surround a room. Maeterlinck himself was only reflecting
the changing philosophical approach to the reality of the
individual self, and to its isolation from other selves. William
James and F. H. Bradley had already tried to answer the
question: "Who am I, and what is the self?" before Beckett
or Pinter. The question: "Who are you?" and the various
individual accounts of themselves given by the characters of
The Collection are sheer Pirandello,* and that is no mean
compliment, for Pirandello is one of the masters of twentieth-
century drama. Everyone has his or her truth, and here I
agree indeed with Paul Mayersberg's views, stated in *The
Listener* of 5 July 1962, that there is nothing absurd in
Pinter's theatre and particularly in *The Collection* in which
every character gives the account which suits him best and
in which he wants to believe for very rationally accountable
psychological motives. Yet again, this play is perhaps a little
contrived and a little too much like a parlour game. Still, in
spite of these slight flaws, it is an entertaining, psychologically
sound play and an easily grasped example of Pinter's method
of creating mystery.

* Hegel and Bergson had dealt with these problems. Barbusse in *L'Enfer*
had described the isolation of the self.

Another play which shows that Pinter can deal, not only with the mechanics of dramatic structure and suspense, but also with psychological reality is *A Night Out*, in which the main character, thoroughly smothered by his mother's over-bearing solicitude, goes out against her will, is haunted by guilt, goes through an extremely well-worked-out scene of guilt-exorcism with a prostitute whom he humiliates as a substitute to his mother, and finally returns back to the maternal yoke. Yet another very skilful display of craftsmanship and psychological knowledge is *A Slight Ache* in which a husband and wife are progressively and subtly transformed under the impact of brooding fear and mystery. The husband breaks down and the wife, fascinated, replaces him by the tramp who has caused the breakdown. Besides this dramatic skill and gift of characterisation, Pinter has a remarkable ear for catching the rhythms of everyday speech and for orchestrating them into very striking cumulative effects.

A far more complex sample of Pinter's dramatic skill and imagination seems to me to be found in his first full length play *The Birthday Party*. This play contains all the influences and ingredients which go into the making of a type of dramatic pattern which Pinter has continued to explore in his subsequent works, and which he had already outlined in his first play, *The Room*. We are, to begin with, in Beckett's land, the land of drama of situation and not of characters. The world is the stage or the room which the protagonists of the drama occupy, and their respective aim is to remain masters of the ground upon which they stand, or masters of the situation. The characters and the dramatic actions which they perform are what they appear to be on the stage, without practically any precedents or prolongations in time. Because of this concentration upon the present, this is therefore a kind of existential theatre. The author professes to be more an observer of the behaviour of his characters than a psychologist who unravels their motives and their actions. The reality of these characters is in fact their dramatic reality, and it is something essentially theatrical. The problem is what kind of reality do they and their actions represent? Is it a profound, meaningful reality which could affectively and intellectually embrace large aspects of humankind, or is it something too sectional, too limited and time bound to be capable of being generalised and universalised into something widely meaningful?

Enthusiastic critics are perhaps overinclined to see too easily correspondences and metaphors embracing the whole human situation, and they construct pseudo-philosophical patterns on rather unsound foundations. We have been told often enough that the world is a stage, that a room can be the image of the world, a tree the image of life, and a man an archetype for a whole section of humankind; yet, it obviously requires a rather dedicated imagination to build up Stan, in *The Birthday Party*, into the image of the failed artist, and Goldberg and McCann into mysterious forces which can dispose of the fate of men. That does not seem to be convincing, for, neither does the psychological make-up of these characters warrant such transmutations, nor do certain naturalistic aspects of the play render them possible, even although Pinter successfully manages to build quite a Kafkaesque atmosphere in the greater part of the play. The flat, cliché-ridden conversation of the first act between Meg, Petey and Stan, who hold the stage until the arrival of the two intruders at the end of the act, is too naturalistic and too socially circumscribed to allow a real atmosphere of mystery, or a climate of unexplainable menace to set in. It is also too reminiscent of Ionesco's *The Bald Prima Donna*, and a small dose of this kind of thing goes a long way. Stan's studied vagueness about his past—he has played once in a concert hall, then *they* (something very ominous and indefinite) carved him up, they shut the hall where he was going to play—is too contrived to pass unnoticed. Stan has not left his papers in Sidcup, but he has certainly left his memory behind him. In the end he will be taken away in a big car which could be a black Maria, an asylum van, or whatever one likes, to Monty who, again, could be anything or anyone one likes. Goldberg and McCann, although they too are rather socially circumscribed for the climate of mystery and unexplainable menace which the play seeks to build up, manage nevertheless to create a kind of atmosphere in which, through meaningless talk and questioning they batter Stan into collapse and dumbness. Had they looked less like gentlemen about town or clubmen on a spree, or had they been less afflicted with social pre-occupations and affiliations, they would have been less definite and more mysterious and terrifying. As it is, they are, like Stan, a bit stagey and the violence which they seek to express is more theatrical than convincing. A simple tap on the arm and Stan rolls on the floor in pain; one hand-hold by Goldberg and McCann is reduced to helplessness.

The atmosphere of menace and lurking terror, which Kafka slowly and progressively builds up in his novels, is more readily understandable in a Europe overwhelmed by fascist regimes and oppression. It is much more difficult to suggest such an atmosphere in countries which have no experience of such calamities. It could probably be done even in plays, but the first prerequisite for that is that a real climate of fear needs to be established before any particular fear could sound convincing. General nouns and indefinite pronouns are not enough to create a climate, and particulars should only be used as embodiments and aspects of universals and not as representations of sectional aspects of society.

It is fully agreed that human behaviour cannot be fully rationalised, and that is at times apparently unpredictable; yet a close and comprehensive analysis could always reveal links between causes and effects, and between potenialities and actions. To suggest, as Pinter does, that the reason why he sometimes knows so little about the logic and motivations of some of his characters, is because these characters allow him to know only so much and no more, or is due to the fact that he has somehow chanced to overhear or to witness only certain aspects of their talk and behaviour, is either to indulge in the mimetic fallacy or to invoke a kind of creative passivity which Pirandello has turned to full account in *Six Characters*, and which is in fact, merely a dramatic device. The truth is that the author makes or allows his characters to be what they are meant to be in accordance with the organic structure and the situation which he has chosen or which has partly imposed itself upon his creativeness. The patches of darkness in a character are therefore wilful or, rather, organic and necessary to the whole; they are like the shadows on a painting; they are not devices or contrivances in order to achieve a given end. Things and actions in art as well as in life are only meaningful in relation to the whole to which they belong, and this relationship must be organic and not conceptual.

The notion, for instance, that one could accept the possibility of a ritual murder* in the naturalistic setting of twentieth-century society with helicopters, lorries and all the other aspects of our scientific age, is difficult to entertain. Whatever ingredients—verbal or otherwise—one might use they cannot create a climate in which ritual murders or re-enactments of the crucifixion could have any truly imaginative reality. The murder which is made to take place in such a background can only be murder pure and simple. Ritual murder can only take place in a social and historical climate in which such a thing is accepted as an integral part of it. The myth of Oedipus has, for twentieth-century man, a meaning different from the one it had for a fifth-century Athenian. The killing of one's father and the marrying of one's mother by twentieth-century man, would not be ascribed to any cosmic, religious punishment but simply to mental derangement. Such deeds could not generate tragic terror and sympathy as they do in Greek tragedies; they could only generate horror and a sense of shame for sordid, bestial acts which could not be looked upon as part of the conflict between men and the gods, and the ground in which the remains of the authors or of the victims of these deeds are buried, is not likely to become hallowed ground, source of divine, beneficent power. No transposition of such actions is possible, except within the entire climate to which they belong. A naturalistic background, or a too well-defined and narrow social context, militates against the supernatural and against universalisation. This is a problem which Pinter has encountered a few times and has never yet fully solved as Beckett has done in

* David Rudkin's play: *Afore Night Comes.*

Waiting for Godot. Yet, all in all, Pinter is more versatile, more gifted, and a better craftsman than any of his contemporary dramatists and he is likely to prove that he has the necessary staying power which will enable him to outdistance most of his contemporaries, with the exception of John Arden.

John Whiting was neither quite contemporary of these young playwrights, nor did he share their main preoccupations with naturalism, social realism, direct artistic commitment or political action. It goes without saying that Pinter, who avoids political and social commitments and action, and concerns himself with his art which certainly aims at transcending naturalism, must not be included in this group. The differences between this group and Whiting account for the latter's partial ostracism from the stage and for his limited success in an age dedicated to attitudes and beliefs which Whiting did not naturally possess or shunned as unworthy of a true artist. That Whiting was such a man, and that the quality and strength of his imagination was superior to any of those who hold the limelight, there should be no doubt about it. *A Penny for a Song* and *Saint's Day* are plays which could not cast discredit on any author, and *Marching Song* should be enough to establish any playwright's reputation, for it shows a remarkable distinction of mind and language—two traits which are anything but the hall-marks of the new wave of dramatists, but which are the prerequisites of important drama. The theme of this play is a large one; it stretches from the historico-social individual represented by a defeated general in quest of his own soul to the nation whose fate is closely connected with his own. The action is taut and compressed in the time limit of thirty-six hours, during which the general must make up his mind either to commit suicide for the good of the state, or stand trial and compel himself and the state to face up to the nakedness of truth, whatever the outcome. The plot is well-knit, and although the characters' ideas could have been clad with perhaps more human substance, they are well enough delineated to be compellingly moving in their respective plights, and in their stumbling attempts to transcend them. The general's character is a bold attempt towards the heroic and towards a confrontation of the problem of human responsibility which men have to face over and over again at the individual level. All in all, setting aside the question of impact and influence based on fluctuating topicality, this seems to me intrinsically the most striking new play of the last decade, excluding, of course, *Waiting for Godot*.

The Devils, which is Whiting's last work, adapted from Huxley's *The Devils of Loudun*, shows that his dramatic skill and mastery of dialogue had developed considerably. Yet, in spite of this most impressive technical progress which compels admiration, *Marching Song* seems to remain a more enriching and more profound experience, and there was ground to hope that if Whiting had been able to match an original and profound theme like that of *Marching Song* with the dramatic skill which he had already displayed, the result would have been a memorable work. His untimely death robs the English stage of this most promising playwright. He had already shown by his mastery of craft and the depth of his vision that he had the making of a major dramatist. These promises which death has frustrated rest for the moment on John Arden on the strength of one single play *Sergeant Musgrave's Dance*, which shows that he has the best poetic imagination at work on the English stage now, and the capacity to counteract the cramping effects of naturalism on that stage. Arden's other plays show versatility and verbal skill but they also underline the fact that unless he works with a theme which carries with it its own inherent dramatic structure, he is apt, as in the case with his last play, *The Workhouse Donkey*, to disperse his efforts into separate pieces of characterisation and actions which pull apart and do not fuse together into the coherence of a dramatic work. Another playwright who has shown that he can handle heroic themes is Robert Bolt whose *A Man for All Seasons* showed a skilful use of Brechtian effects and a well-integrated blend of historical data and modernity. The moving plight of Sir Thomas More, admirably portrayed by Paul Scofield, made of this play a remarkable achievement.

The naturalism and social preoccupation which weigh perhaps too heavily on the English stage at this moment make themselves felt even in productions and in acting. One example will suffice, it is the new *Othello* production at the Old Vic.

The subtitle of *Othello* is *The Moor of Venice*. The plot of the play is from Guido Cinthio's novel *Il Moro di Venezia*. *Moro*, as an adjective, means dark skinned or dark haired as is proved by the countless patronymic names of Mori, Moro, Moretti, etc. The *Mori*, in the Mediterranean world, from Spain to Italy are the Moors, generally dark skinned and dark haired, but not the blacks or the negroes. In the eighth century the Moors or Arabs conquered the Mediterranean world, right up to the south of France, where they were halted in 742, and remained in Spain until 1492. The Moors were great warriors, admired and feared by their enemies. The negroes were only used as slaves by the Moors and the substitution of one for the other is historically more than doubtful. The only negroes known in fifteenth-century Venice were likely to be slaves sold by the Moors. Courage, passionate temper, jealousy about women fit the Moors. The description of Othello as dark and sooty is understandable if one compares him with the much talked about fairness of the Venetians. His thick lips could very well be a distortion of Iago, but they could also very well be so without making of him a negro. A Moor war leader is, owing to the ascendancy of the Moors in the fifteenth century, quite within the climate of the time, a negro general at that time and in that context, is unthinkable.

Olivier chooses to play Othello as if he were a negro. He not only covers himself in black soot from top to toe, he has crinkly hair, a drooping lower lip, gaping open pink tongue and roseate palate and eyes skilfully rolling between white and red. Besides that, he has adopted the bare-feet, hip-rolling or slouching ways of walking or standing of negroes. His speech is appropriately guttural, yodelling, lisping or syncopated according to circumstances, except in rare, though welcome, moments, when he lapses into his most effective natural voice.

The part of Othello seems to be the most emotionally exacting of the Shakespearean theatre. Those of Lear and Hamlet which are longer and more complex and profound, do not carry the same purely emotional scope and intensity. The only part which seems to compare with it in that domain, if that of Phèdre. Olivier rises to the part and gives a unique display of emotional vitality and stamina which rides wave upon wave of passion to finally produce the tidal flood which lifts up in a mighty flow which leaves one astonished as when at the end of Scene 3 Act III, Othello unfolds the majestic:

> O blood, blood, blood! ...
> Never Iago. Like the Pontic sea
> Whose icy currents and compulsive course...

There is no doubt that this is a great performance, worthy of a very great actor, unlikely to be surpassed in our time; yet it seems to me to fall short of the tragic grandeur of the part and for various reasons, most of them connected with the conception of the play.

The mechanics of the plot, the means by which the author and Iago goad Othello to murder and self-destruction rest upon jealousy, and there is no doubt that unless jealousy is of an implacable awe-inspiring nature, it can, as is often the case, turn into laughter and melodrama. Othello's jealousy, in its growth and demented final explosion, conforms perfectly with the more profound aspects of human psychology and is as true as that of Phèdre or Hermione. Othello's simple, passionate, sensuous nature coupled with the social differences which mark him from Desdemona, is a preordained prey to jealousy. The fact that Desdemona has thrown all ties and restraints to the wind for the love of him convinces him that she could do so again if she loved another man. Yet, however much the growth and unfolding of Othello's jealousy may conform to psychological truth as we know it, the dramaturgical problem lies in the means used in order to give it birth and to bring it to its final explosion. That problem which is coincidental with the mechanism of the plot, concerns particularly Iago. To look upon him as D. Leavis suggests, as a weak, incidental piece of machinery, or as a kind of vocal aspect of Othello's subconscious is to unbalance the tragedy and to scale it down uncomfortably close to the borderland of melodrama. That Othello's receptivity and propensity to jealousy and rash behaviour are as important as Iago's intellectual mastery and persuasiveness nobody doubts. One can easily see that the latter carefully nurses and brings to a final conflagration embers which were already dimly glowing in the dark psyche of Othello. But to do that requires not only intellect, perspicacity, convincing powers and a manipulating skill, but also either a terrifying thirst for destruction and self-destruction, or a reckless urge to go to the limits of experience.*

A Iago who is a mere piece of machinery to unleash emotion runs the risk of turning these emotions into inflated rhetoric which only the steel frame of the sense of the metaphysical could sustain and transform into heart-rending displays of human sorrows. Intense feelings and emotions which are either merely provoked by devices, or have no aura of transcendence beyond the present and the purely human, have, because of that, their wings clipped, and they can only rise to limited heights. Besides that, neither Othello nor any man can be all in one, an equilibrated compound of the acme of Being and of Non-Being. Lucifer himself was only each in turns, not at the same time. Iago is the greatest incarnation of evil in Western art, Mephistopheles excepted, since he is a direct manifestation of the supernatural. Macbeth is not fully evil: he indulges in it partly incidentally, by ambition and influenced by his wife. Goetz in Sartre's play *Le Diable et le Bon Dieu* only used evil as a means to challenge God for whom he obviously longs. Iago's evil behaviour and actions are totally in excess of his human motives, and that is where they bear the mark of true evil. They are a blind, unfathomable denial of the Good. Neither his dis-

* See note at the end of chapter.

appointed ambition, nor the untested and unproven suggestion that the Moor might have done his office "betwixt his
sheets" can account for the destructive urge which gnaws at
his heart. Unless Iago is a terrifying incarnation of evil the
bed load of dead at the end of the play and his cold ruthless
rejection of Desdemona's desperate plea on the edge of death
are deprived of the scaffolding of metaphysical terror which
makes the difference between tragic death, incommensurate
with any human deserts, and contingent death which could
have been avoided. In this age of repudiation of heroes,
demythologising and pseudo-Marxism, tragedy and metaphysics, which go together, are cold-shouldered; yet *Othello*
is a tragedy, and a superficial, trickstery Iago engrossed in his
puppetry games can only underline the blindness and extreme
simplicity of both Othello and Desdemona. The one seems
to be so intent in cultivating his jealousy, and the other is
made to appear so naïvely innocent, so incompetent that even
when her husband is obviously distraught by jealousy and
anger at the discovery of the loss of the semi-magic handkerchief, she can only soothe him with the name of Cassio. In
fact her single-mindedness to the task of keeping Cassio's
name in her husband's ears, whatever the place and the
occasion, while their honeymoon has barely been completed,
can only be glossed over and looked upon as a mere incident
in the making of a great tragedy, if the style of performance
is entirely non-naturalistic and if Iago's daemonic powers are
so terrifyingly convincing as to obnubilate any form of
naturalistic criticism.

To present Othello as a well-defined member of a social
stratum and to have him act naturalistically as the representative of a given racial or social group is to break the overall
style and so unbalance the play. Not only is there no historical
reason for looking upon him as a negro, but the playing of the
part with all the refinements of the negro's speech and behaviour can only cause one to wonder why the Venetians are
not played as Venetians and Cypriots as Cypriots. If Othello
is to be particularised to the point of naturalistic verisimilitude, then Desdemona and Cassio should be presented as

Venetians and not as products of English education. This would not improve the play; far from it, but it would at least maintain a uniformity of style. Othello's epilepsy needs neither to be photographically real nor capped by a dagger in the mouth of the stretched body, something which looks rather sensational and phallic. Neither does Cassio need to be sent sprawling to the floor to show what a low, undignified commander he is, in a scene of much kissing and belly-dancing. Although Desdemona is said by Iago to hold Cassio's palm, it is surely not necessary that each time that Othello sets eyes on her and Cassio they should be holding hands, for this becomes as faintly comical and forced as Iago's account of the night when Cassio lay abed with him, kissing him, passing his leg over him, and calling him sweet names as if he were Desdemona. The scene of the fight between Cassio and Roderigo and the death of the latter could be less protracted so as to avoid any risk of making of it an anti-climax to the great death scene of the end.

Othello is, of all the great tragedies, the most dramatic. The end here is not so clearly in the beginning as it is in *Lear* or in *Hamlet*; neither is it a progressive revelation of unbearable knowledge which finally offers death as the only possible solution. Othello has in himself the seeds of his tragedy, yet they must grow and develop through actions and reactions, along a line of mounting tension to the catastrophe of the end. The psychological verisimilitude of these actions and the particularism which play a far more important part here than in *Hamlet* or *Lear*, can easily lead to naturalistic over-emphasis or to sheer inflation if they are not counterbalanced by the substratum of evil which is part of Iago's character. Sir Laurence Olivier's great feat of characterisation, although perhaps misguided in its goal, deserves the highest praise for artistic skill and for a splendid solo performance, even when hip swaying, yodelling and jazz dancing, he sometimes comes uncomfortably close to the guying of the part which he has chosen to present. These failings cannot but take away some of the nobility and tragic grandeur which Sir Laurence could

easily have brought to the part, had there been less naturalism and particularism of Othello's social roots, and a greater
ontological depth in the concept of the character of Iago.

It would not be possible to conclude a study of the main
trends of contemporary drama without saying a few words
about Joan Littlewood and the workshop theatre, and about
the Royal Shakespeare Company, directed by Peter Hall.
There are few examples of a more complete dedication to
the type of theatre in which she believes than that of Joan
Littlewood. After the war, she set about touring the country
with the aim of bringing the theatre to the people. She had
a very hard struggle which tested to the full her idealism
and that of her company. In 1953, she found a home at the
Royal Theatre, Stratford at the Bow, and after a slow, painful beginning, she began to achieve fame with Brendan
Behan's first play, *The Quare Fellow*, in 1956, which was
followed by a series of striking successes like *The Hostage* by
the same author, *A Taste of Honey* by Shelagh Delaney,
Fings Ain't Wot They Used T'Be by Frank Norman and other
plays which were all transferred to the West End.

Joan Littlewood, the best-known exponent of Brechtian
staging in England, is a dab hand at turning a sketch or an
inchoate script into an entertaining blend of songs, dances
and topicalities. There is no doubt that the plays mentioned
above owe most of their success to her dynamic, inventive
talents, and that her absence at Stratford at the Bow was
sadly felt and her return with the play *What a Lovely War*
was a triumphal success which shows that she is one of the
most versatile and vital producers of the world. *What a Lovely
War* is one of the most exciting and moving experiences of
modern drama; it is a masterly scenic presentation of man's
follies and sorrows, and it both sears and cleanses the heart.
Transcending national differences and personal conflicts,
Joan Littlewood has grappled with the universal theme of the
pity and the tragedy of war, and she has done so without any
traces of the kind of proselytism, social preaching or dogmatism which mar a play like *The Representative*. She has
produced a complete and fully rounded picture of the stupid-

ity, egoism, hypocrisy, greed and irrepressible courage and
resilience of the human animal. Far more effectively than
any C.N.D. march, vague allegories about human conformism
and loss of Eden, or sectional representations of the class war
this musical-morality, which so convincingly outlines the
inanity of wars and the need for human brotherhood, takes
its place with Beckett's *Waiting for Godot* as one of the high-
lights of the contemporary theatre.

The Royal Shakespeare Company, based in London, in the
Aldwych Theatre, and unrivalled from the point of view of
acting talents, has been responsible for some of the most remarkable productions which London has seen in the last few
years. Working on a repertory basis makes it possible to have
the smallest parts played by very accomplished actors, and also
to avoid the usual staleness of interpretation which descends
upon any production which has a long run. Among the productions at the Aldwych, those which stand out are Anouilh's
Becket, John Whiting's *The Devils*, Chekov's *The Seagull*,
Brecht's *The Caucasian Chalk Circle*, and the most memorable
of all, Peter Brook's production of *King Lear* in which Paul
Scofield, the outstanding tragic actor of this age, gives a render-
ing of Lear which is not likely to be outshone in our time or
forgotten in the history of drama.

* In a letter to *The Times*, 15th Oct., 1964, Professor Peter Wilson complained
that he could discover no dignity in the main character and concluded with
the words: "Must we give up Shakespeare's heroes? Must we refuse to admit
that the basis of his tragedy was his belief in the integrity of Man?"

CHAPTER SIX

DRAMA IN THE U.S.A.

O'NEILL wrote and produced most of his plays before the second world war, but five of them, among which his two best—*The Long Day's Journey Into Night* and *The Iceman Cometh*—were produced for the first time between 1946 and 1960 and are therefore part of the period under study. The three other plays recently produced, *Hughie* and particularly *A Moon for the Misbegotten* and *A Touch of the Poet* are also worthy of O'Neill. *Mourning becomes Electra* was recently given a striking production at the Old Vic in London which left no doubt about this play's greatness. *Desire under the Elms* was revived and also made into a successful film. All these plays have added greatly to the reputation and influence of O'Neill. Besides that, there is the important and decisive fact for this study that we are, at this moment, in the middle of an O'Neill revival which shows that his reputation is approaching the status which it ought to have and which is that he is, with Claudel and Brecht, one of the three greatest dramatists of the twentieth century. Claudel is a greater genius than either, only equalled by Yeats, but O'Neill is possibly a more prolific and varied playwright than any one of these mentioned, even although he is not a poet on the same scale as Claudel, Yeats or even Brecht. Still, whatever one may think of these tentative assessments which are obviously arguable, the fact remains that *Mourning becomes Electra, The Long Day's Journey Into Night, The Iceman Cometh, Galileo, Mother Courage, The Chalk Circle, Le Soulier de Satin, Partage de Midi, l'Annonce faite à Marie, Murder in the Cathedral, The Family Reunion* and *Waiting for Godot* are among the great plays of our time.

O'Neill's work has been extensively examined, and as a

great deal of it lies outside the scope of this study it will not be mentioned. Yet, since tragedy and the possibilities of tragedy in modern times play such a vital part in it, it might seem remiss and utterly inappropriate not to mention one of the most important attempts at tragedy in modern times simply because it was first produced in 1936. This is *Mourning becomes Electra*, a play which has been thoroughly discussed, analysed, praised or denigrated on the ground that it is neither Greek nor modern and that the plot, shorn of its Greek climate of fate and inexorable gods, is merely a sordid *crime passionnel*, followed by revenge, which is the stock-in-trade of the sensational press. Then, if one looks at it from such an angle, so is *Phèdre* and so is *Andromaque*. But the question is, can one adopt such an attitude? And the answer certainly is no, unless, of course, one is intent in pulling these plays to pieces. True enough, Racine does not transpose Greek tragedy in a modern, or near-modern setting; he merely deals with an ancient Greek myth as a seventeenth-century writer. Therefore, there is a fundamental difference between his approach to Greek myth and that of O'Neill who uses the framework of Greek plays to put on it a modern, very modern, theme, since, although the action is set in the American Civil War, the motives of the action are thoroughly Freudian.

It is indeed a far cry from the Mennons to the Atrides, and the curse of fate is here replaced by all the possible permutations of incestuous love. No doubt these motives are laboured and are over-obvious; no doubt the machinery is at times creaking, for O'Neill transposes very closely and detail by detail; no doubt also the crimes of Clytemnestra and Orestes are part of a religious world which, with its strict rules and rituals, practically guided the hands which committed them. Therefore these characters are truly the victims of forces, or of a form of transcendence which overwhelms them. In that respect they reach a tragic grandeur which can only be attained in similar conditions, that is to say in the Greek world where man pitted his will and his courage against fate and gods which he knew were bound to overwhelm him. Such is not the case with O'Neill's world in which religion has been replaced by psychology. O'Neill is certainly religious and as much obsessed by sin and guilt as any Greek tragedian, but the Christian God cannot be made to intervene to unleash violence, murder and revenge on creation, as could the inhabitants of the Greek Olympus; so that O'Neill has to replace ancestral fury and religious revenge by Freudian psychology. The temperature at which the dramatic fusion takes place is therefore, to start with, definitely lower, and it can never be raised to the same heights through the means which O'Neill uses. Nevertheless, it certainly is raised very high, and that is done by the sheer human violence of the passions involved. Orin and Lavinia are not the descendants of the Atrides, they are only the children of an American general, yet the single-mindedness, the violence with which they tear each other to pieces is both terrifying and piteous. Why, why do that? Because cruel nature has put into them incestuous, hateful forces which can only explode and destroy those who harbour them. It is neither regal nor ritualistic, but it is terribly human, and as the human is the very basis of regality and ritualism, they therefore go a long way towards the requirements of tragedy. Those who cannot be impressed by the imaginative range which, throughout the whole sequence of three plays, was able practically to hold together the two sets of situations and transpose one in terms of the other, are perhaps over stretching their critical faculties. It seems to me that in spite of weaknesses, particularly in the third part of the trilogy which of necessity is weak, since there cannot be any Minerva, Areopagus or redemption, and in spite also of defects previously mentioned, this is an achievement on a grand scale and, of its kind, unsurpassed in twentieth-century drama. The measure of O'Neill's failure in this respect is the measure of the lack of spirituality of our society and of its incapacity to apprehend works of wide-ranging imagination, which instead of plodding heavily along the ground as art is supposed to do now, soar towards regions which the short-sighted dismiss as cloud-ridden and illusory.

It is not only O'Neill who is found incongenial to our social-realism obsessed society, it is also Aeschylus who is dismissed on practically similar grounds, because Orestes does not speak the language of Jimmy Porter and Beatie Briant. Their cry is: What is Electra to me or what is Hecuba to me? Hamlet knew better and he could draw the lesson. As Boileau said apropos of La Fontaine, "Nos beaux esprits ont beau se trémousser, ils n'effacerout pas le bonhomme." The same can be said about the author of *Mourning becomes Electra*. There are in *Mourning becomes Electra* touches of melodrama, because O'Neill stands too clearly behind the characters and obviously directs the mechanism of their actions through some of his obsessions with Freudianism which are mostly concerned with sex. Besides that, the language lacks, of course, "the rise, the roll, the creation"; but then, had he had that gift also, he would have been a great poet; without it, he still is a great dramatist in spite of his stylistic shortcomings and poetic limitations.

Desire under the Elms is another aspect of O'Neill's attempt at tragedy. This time there is no transposition from Greek plays, it is, on the contrary, a piece of stark realism, with unbearable ancestral forces which compel violence and terror. The characters lack grandeur, but they certainly move in an atmosphere of tragedy. Among the plays which were produced in recent years, *The Long Day's Journey Into Night* is probably O'Neill's most accomplished play and a near masterpiece in its genre. No writer has succeeded better than O'Neill in dramatising his own inner conflicts, tensions and family quarrels. Compared with it, the attempts made by Tennessee Williams with *The Glass Menagerie* or Osborne with *Look Back in Anger* are child's stammerings. The image of the pelican feeding his own brood with his own entrails has always seemed to me extremely untidy and pretty revolting, albeit it was one of the chosen symbols of romantic poetry. O'Neill proceeds with the vision of a poet and the cool skilful hand of a master surgeon. It is all done as it looks in Rembrandt's famous painting, and the operation itself becomes a work of art; the blood, the entrails are transmuted into symbols which act on the imagination and not on the sentiments. Whatever we feel, we feel it through imagination and not through directly apprehended emotions, and if we shed tears, they are tears which act like quicksilver on base metal and turn it to gold. After such an experience we are different. O'Neill follows the dramatist whom he admired so much—Strindberg, in conveying emotions through intensity and concentration and in carefully avoiding flailing gestures and dispersions. The quartet of *The Long Day's Journey* are caught in the Nessian cloth of their respective loves, hates and fears, and each move any one of them makes tears the skin apart, causes the blood to flow, and brings death nearer. Every attempt at truce and embrace ends in a fierce struggle from which the two protagonists emerge more bruised than before. And so, the soul-destroying wastage of human love and fumbling compassion continues until, in the end, every unfortunate member of this family has practically succeeded, with his own efforts and with the help of his dearest, in wrapping himself up in his own shroud. This is one of the most profound, most human plays of the world drama, and no-one can watch it or read it without coming out of such an experience, chastened and filled with sympathy, admiration and deep pity for the human condition.

The Iceman Cometh, first produced in 1946, is, in spite of its repetitiousness, padding and incoherence, a great play. It is O'Neill's great parable of life and a morality play, imaging the human condition; it is a vast Breughelian fresco in which men grope about in a kind of dazed alcoholic stupor, under the shadow of the Iceman—Death. It is a kind of Dance of death, in which men, overwhelmed by guilt, try in vain to shelter in illusions so as not to face the truth, and generally end in killing the thing they love because they are all too aware that they cannot love enough. It is Gorki's *Lower Depths* with a sin-ridden humankind which can neither forget nor rid itself of the sense of guilt and failure. Instead of Beckett's tramps waiting for Godot, we have here a whole room full of down-and-outs in Hope's Saloon bar, in a state of drunken stupor and waiting for Hickey who comes every now and then to plunge them into a wild binge and to make them completely forget their twilight or limbo world of vague

139

dreams and notions of joys, happiness, loyalties and affections. They vaguely entertain such notions through the fumes of alcohol for they vaguely know that if the fumes dissipated, and they were made to face up to truth or reality, they could not, for it is both too tinged with evil and too close to death for which they unconsciously long. "To hell with the truth!" says Larry, "as the history of the world proves, the truth has no bearings on anything. It's irrelevant and immaterial as the lawyers say. The lie of a pipe dream is what gives life to the whole misbegotten, mad lot of us, drunk or sober." They can only go on living at the cost of making their consciousness dead, for, if it were allowed to awaken it would show them that they were murderous animals filled with hatred and desires for self-destruction. They are therefore condemned to live as Sartre says "in bad faith", in duplicity, for if they awaken they know that they are all guilty. The drunken stupor does not hide here a truth which they do not want to face up to, as is the case with Brick in *Cat on a Hot Tin Roof*; it hides their longings for death because of their inescapable corruption, something which is part of the human condition.

Those who speak of this kind of fundamental pessimism in condemnatory tones, could easily extend to Kierkegaard, Pascal, Luther and Augustine the very same blame. Yet this is the pessimism of those who know that, however fallen, guilty and tormented man may be, there is a love, a peace and a form of hope which passes human understanding and which he can achieve if he trusts, not in illusions, false pride, bad faith and lies, but in true love, in the love which forgives all as Christ forgave all that was done against him. The moment Hickey realises that he has killed his wife, not to save her from further suffering, but because he hated her and could no longer bear her unfailing forgiveness and the purity of her love, he realises his true guilt and surrenders as a murderer so as to pay for his crime. He realises that he was mad. Parrit and Larry, who are both transformed by Hickey's discovery of truth, can no longer face life. Parrit, realising that he is guilty of his mother's murder, kills himself, and Larry prepares for death with the words: "the best of all were never to be born". The other bunch of Hope's establishment, who, through lack of grace or vision, cannot grasp the truth of Hickey's confession, merely fasten upon his words: "I must have been crazy", and go back to their drinks and illusions.

The pessimism we find in this play is that of a profoundly religious man and it is a pessimism which does not exclude redemption and hope. *Waiting for Godot* does not exclude hope either, but Beckett's subsequent plays, *End Game, Krapp's Last Tape* which ends with the words: "I would have them (my days) again" and *Happy Days* plunge deep into nihilism where hope, though not courage, has practically died, and where human life is partially paralysed and at its last gasp. Tennessee William's neurotic pessimism is above all the result of sexual obsessions and maladjustments, and when it is not grounded in social conflicts and characterisations, as is the case with *A Streetcar named Desire*, it turns into purely superficial agitation and sensationalism. It is pessimism without deep foundations. The same conclusions apply to Anouilh whose intellectual brilliance, dashing style and dramatic skill enable him to juggle with men's plight, sorrow and failures as if they were part of a vast game in which, as long as they get their mead of applause for their performance, it does not matter much whether or not Arlequin's tears and worries are real and deeply grounded in the consciousness of his plight, or are merely a game.

To compare *The Iceman Cometh* with Tennessee Williams's faltering attempts at universality with *Camino Real*, or *The Long Day's Journey into Night* with *Cat on a Hot Tin Roof* by the same author, is to make clear at once the difference between genius and talent. The failures and flaws of genius are of a different nature from those pertaining to talent. *Camino Real*, for instance, exhibits the failure of the author's imagination which cannot hold together the disparate elements which it tries to fuse into a vast mythical panorama of the life of man. *Cat on a Hot Tin Roof* is earthbound and much circumscribed by crudities and by the limitations of the characters involved. The failures of genius are, on the contrary, failures of abundance, exuberance and lack of measure, they are the cacophonous noises of a heavenly concert or the dark patches in an otherwise dazzling light. Every one of O'Neill's best plays has flaws. *Mourning becomes Electra* is at times melodramatic and laboured, *The Iceman Cometh* suffers from prolixity and lack of clarity, and *The Long Day's Journey Into Night* suffers from touches of rawness, but these flaws do not prevent any one of these plays from being a great play. Whatever the method followed, O'Neill tries in each of these cases to reach for the universal. In the first, he starts from a universal theme in which he has to infuse the kind of contemporary life which links it with perenniality. In the second he starts from the particular, from the basic reality of life in America at a given time, to break the mould and overflow into a vast epic of mankind. In the third, he starts from various selves and members of his family, all guilt-ridden seekers for a kind of identity and peace which they long for, and he rises to the universal plight of man in search of his soul and heaven, and clawing and tearing to shreds himself and everyone with whom he associates, while showing throughout such a high and noble capacity for suffering and for enduring that it becomes the very basis of man's greatness.

After O'Neill, both Tennessee Williams and Arthur Miller, who are America's most important living dramatists, seem quite average, yet, both have already won well-deserved high places in the roll-call of world drama. Tennessee Williams seems to be the more fecund and varied of the two; he even seems to have the edge on Miller in technical skill, in which, among living playwrights, he is only surpassed by Anouilh. The world of Tennessee Williams is a world of lonely individuals with morbid, maladjusted sensibilities in quest of forms of happiness which they cannot reach. There is no God they could appeal to and no society which will end their inhibitions and redress their wrongs. They carry these wrongs in themselves, and the part played by society is slight even in plays like *The Glass Menagerie* or *A Streetcar named Desire*. Through drugs, drinks and reckless living, the idealists and neurotics of Tennessee Williams seem to be intent upon self-destruction. The world is too much for them; time, the destroyer, disintegrates and wipes away purity, innocence and beauty. We are in Anouilh's territory which is also the territory of necrophilic romanticism in which men struggle in vain to shake off the hand of fate or the iron chains of circumstances which weigh heavily upon them. Blanche Dubois is caught in the illusion of her past and her dreams, and she cannot live in the world in which she finds herself. The sensitive individuals of Tennessee Williams are not unlike Anouilh's. They cannot face up to time and to reality, and life defeats them. Laura, Blanche and Kilroy are relations of Thérèse in *La Sauvage*, of Antigone or Joan of Arc; they cannot reconcile their idealism with the realities of life. The author, although he sympathises with their dreams and failures, has enough awareness of reality to remain quite objective, even in his most autobiographical play—*The Glass Menagerie* which is his *Long Day's Journey Into Night*.

The Glass Menagerie is among Williams's best plays and it is a good play, but compared with *Long Day's Journey Into Night*, with its sombre, relentless, tragic atmosphere and the violence and grandeur of the search for roots and true responsibilities, it remains a delicate, frail, exquisite exploration of a world riddled with whimsies and deprived of grandeur and gripping reality. The mother's dreams of gracious living and her refusal to face up to the fact that the world in which she lives has neither time nor patience for her illusions of gentility and for her crippled daughter, have the same effects on her children as the Tarde family on Thérèse. The son Tom, like Willy Loman, lives in deceit and lies because he dares not confess the truth, and in the end he can only free himself by following in his father's footsteps, that is to say by running away. Every member of this family is a failure engaged in a hopeless rearguard action against reality, at times unredeemed by stretches of pseudo-poetic language. *A Streetcar named Desire*, which deals with the same social theme, is a much better play and possibly Williams's best. Blanche, the heroine, is a much more real and human character than any of the characters of *The Glass Managerie*.

She too clings to her dreams and illusions and refuses to face the facts, but she does so because she is too lonely and because she is unable to live without her illusions. She tries to deaden her dreams with crude sexuality, and it is of course sexuality which completes her destruction. She is an anachronism in Stanley Kowaleski's world in which both her sister and her husband are quite happy in their animality, and Blanche's attempts to awaken them to the truth of their debased life is fiercely resisted by Stanley who, if ever her views triumphed, would be completely dethroned. So, he sets about to destroy her with the same means with which he subdued her sister and which Blanche herself has already tried in vain—sex. He rapes her and thus completes the breakdown which sends her to the asylum, out of a society in which she cannot live. She clearly stands condemned from the beginning; there is no room for her in our modern society. She is therefore, up to a point, a victim, yet her death and destruction, sad as they may be, and they are so, leave behind them an impression of hopeless waste, due to the fact that they are totally useless. Blanche is pathetic in her attempt to transcend loneliness with all sorts of means, but never tragic; she is a trapped human being, lacking nobility and the self-awareness of her plight.

With these two plays the pattern of Tennessee Williams about illusions and sex is firmly set. Alma in *Summer and Smoke* dreams like Laura of a normal married life, including a sex life, but that cannot be for she is too frightened of the body. Serafina in *The Rose Tattoo* has on the contrary made of the body a fetish; for her, sex is all. She is an inflated, rather unreal and melodramatic female Stanley Kowaleski, who rhapsodizes about sex in typical Tennessee Williams pseudo-poetic style. *Cat on a Hot Tin Roof* continues to show the same obsession with sex in a pretty sentimental and unconvincing manner. Maggie's attempts to get her husband in bed with her are crude and based on low mercenary motives. Much too much is made of the possibilities of a single act of copulation, and the play lacks coherence of movement. None of the characters is in the last resort sympathetic; they are all intent on their self-interests and neuroses. In spite of a great deal of talk about truth, none of the characters is without his lies. The only truly sincere relationship is that which unites father and son; its break-up is both moving and pathetic, but Brick is a confirmed escapist and he remains unchanged. Brick is like Val in *Orpheus Descending*, a typical specimen of feminine man dear to Tennessee Williams; Kilroy in *Camino Real* is another. They are the opposite of the Kowaleskis and Big Daddies, they do not want to give in to women, and they are in fact both male and female. Lady, the woman for whom Val falls, is a weaker Serafina (both parts have been admirably played by the same actress—Anna Magnani), and Jube is like Big Daddy, lecherous and afflicted with cancer. Orpheus-Val is like Anouilh's Orpheus, dreaming of purity, of washing away the stains of corruption in some Lethean river of non-commitment and freedom, and he ends in being torn to bits not by the Maenads, but by dogs; a very melodramatic, highly coloured retelling of the Orpheus myth.

Yet Tennessee Williams had not finished with the myth of the poet which, as is the case with Cocteau, whose poetic self-consciousness he shares, seems to obsess him. He returned to it with *Suddenly Last Summer*. Here we are again in the steamy, decadent South, in a mansion which looks as if it had been invaded by tropical jungle. The Orpheus who used to live in it was a maladjusted homosexual called Sebastian, who used to go abroad with his mother to write one poem a year. He obviously is as dependent on his mother as Laura is on hers, and as soon as he is free from her presence, he indulges openly his homosexuality, using his cousin Catherine who accompanied him, as a bait. Having sinned and feeling guilty, he must pay, he must atone through suffering and death; so, dressed in white, ready for the sacrifice (Tennessee Williams's symbolism is generally as obvious as Cocteau's) he goes out into the street where children are playing ritualistic music. There, all is white, waiting for the immolation of the guilty poet who composes his last poem by sacrificing himself to the evil of the universe. This is a pretty far-fetched piece of poetical fantasy and highly undisguised symbolism. Yet in spite of all that, the myth of Orpheus is anything but dead in

Tennessee Williams. Having spanned the whole of his literary career from *Battle of Angels* in 1940, to *Orpheus Descending* in 1957 and *Suddenly Last Summer* in 1958, he reappears again with *Sweet Bird of Youth* in 1959. This time Orpheus is called Chance Wayne; he is a gigolo in search of his lost innocence and living with a beautiful actress called Alexandra who is a direct relation of Mrs. Karen Stone of *The Roman Spring of Mrs. Stone*. Chance Wayne is hunting in vain the sweet bird of youth which has disappeared for good, in spite of Chance's attempt to coax it back to life. The actress uses him as a drug to give herself the illusion of youth, but illusions cannot be stretched too far on the Procrustean bed of reality, or they break. Sex is no substitute for love, and the two bed partners leave each other in their own solitudes. Chance's sexual relationship with a young woman of his native town to which he has not returned have infected that young woman with venereal disease and the father, a kind of ferocious Big Daddy, plans revenge. He will satisfy his Oedipus complex by having Chance castrated. Tennessee Williams, as the French say, *"n'y va pas avec le dos de la cuillère"*, and although we are in the 1960's, with him, cannibalism and castration go on as in the good old days, while his symbolism has generally the advantage of being extra clear. He probably remembers Cocteau's advice that the poetry of the theatre should be good, visible thick rope, and he makes use of it. The result is often sheer sensationalism, melodrama with jostling blacks and whites, and shallow characterisation due to oversimplification and lack of contact with reality.

Arthur Miller, on the contrary, keeps a very close contact with reality, and his plays are directly in the line of Ibsen's socially conscious drama. In fact, he obviously loves Ibsen so much that he has rewritten for him an *Enemy of the People*, which is as happy a transformation as Cocteau's adaptations of Sophocles or of Shakespeare. His best play is *Death of a Salesman* with its famous character Willy Loman. As Arthur Miller has argued about the tragic character of Wily Loman in the preface to his collected plays, and as his play clearly illustrates the differences between tragedy and social drama, his point of view will be briefly examined. The first point to note is that Willy Loman all too obviously belongs to a clearly defined and very circumscribed society in which values are commercial success and salesmanship, and thus his failure as a salesman is also his undoing. Now, this of course is a real and very earnest theme pertaining to our modern world, and particularly to American society, yet, it must be said that the ideal of being a good salesman, or of outdoing all the Joneses around oneself, can hardly be called a worthy, and least of all, a noble, idea. Will Loman is a pathetic, sentimental, at times, laughable and even vulgar little man who has not grown up. "Dad", he says, "left when I was such a boy I still feel kind of temporary about myself." He has not rid himself of his childish dreams of going into the jungle of life and coming out of it with the winning prize in his hands. His son, who has failed to give life to his dreams and who, through his discovery of his trivial affair with a woman, has contributed to the shattering of the picture that he was trying to build of himself, has become part of his obsession to justify himself through him and to him. His dream, the dream of the commercial society he lives in, is to be a successful man, and as he cannot achieve such a dream, he resorts to all sorts of pathetic lies to cling to the illusion that this dream is about to come true. Only the fact that he is obviously mentally deranged and on the verge of complete collapse can excuse his forcing of his son to lie so as not to completely destroy his own illusions. The product of a debased, heartless, mechanical society, he has tried in vain to conform to its laws and standards, and, as he has been unable to succeed, he has involved his whole family in his lack of moral courage to accept the responsibility of his own failure. In spite of the noble support of his wife, who has far more moral fibre than he has, he ends in a suicide which, although of good intent towards his wife, is still a pitiful refusal to face up to his responsibilities, and is also a final piece of salesmanship, since he is wilfully trying to cheat his insurance company.

Arthur Miller's earnestness and passionate desire to point

out and to correct the weaknesses and injustices of a society based on material rewards and success, though they have resulted in a remarkable social drama, cannot unfortunately compensate for the lack of clarity of his argumentation in the preface of his plays, or for the confusion of aims which somehow mars the wholeness of his play and prevents it from rising to the height where he would like to place it. At the beginning of his preface he begins by stating in a rather grandiloquent and condescending manner, that: "as a writer of plays . . . I lack both the scholarly patience and the zeal to define terms in such a way as to satisfy everyone." Patience and zeal are attributes of the will, therefore one might or one might not display them, without in any way abetting a jot of one's claims to intellectual importance. Yet clarity of thinking, not only in defining terms but also in ascertaining and differentiating between categories or between motives and compulsions, is certainly not a matter of zeal; neither are these discriminations pure and simple academic questions. To compare the law of success with the moral law against incest or that which compelled Antigone to bury her dead brother is to show a singular lack of "zeal and patience". The same applies to the analogy between Aristotle and Euclid. "Aristotle having spoken of a fall from the heights, it goes without saying that someone of the common world cannot be a fit tragic hero. It is now many centuries since Aristotle lived. There is no more reason for falling down in a faint before his *Poetics* than before Euclid's geometry, which has been amended numerous times by men with new insights; nor for that matter would I choose to have my illness diagnosed by Hippocrates rather than the most ordinary graduate of an American medical school, despite the Greek's genius. Things do change and even a genius is limited by his time and the nature of his society." (Arthur Miller, Preface to his collected plays, p. 32. Cresset Press.)

Aesthetic truth is certainly relative, as relative as scientific truth, yet they are not ascertained by the same means, therefore they are not analogous. Aristotle's aesthetics and ethics may be challenged and even repudiated, yet not by the same incontrovertible scientific laws which apply to the case of Euclidian geometry. Aesthetic laws are not invalidated by scientific discoveries in the way in which Hippocrates' knowledge is invalidated by modern medical progress. They are not in fact laws, they are pragmatic deductions from patterns and structures of art, verified by experience which can no doubt be argued about, but which, once they are transposed according to the social-historical context in which they are applied, have not lost their structural validity. Genius, and Aristotle was a genius of the first magnitude, is not intrinsically limited by the time and by the nature of the society in which he lives. The core of truth which Plato, Shakespeare or Dante expressed is not bound by the age in which they lived. What strictly pertained to their respective ages, and is therefore ephemeral, are such things as the conventions, the mental structures and analogies or the historico-social data which they used as the framework of the truths which they expressed; but these fundamental truths will remain valid as long as the civilisation to which they belong retains some form of life. Mr. Miller seems inclined to think that the map of spiritual knowledge is submitted to the same fluctuations as the map of scientific knowledge or data, something which should not be equated with certain fundamental scientific principles which, although only verified in modern times, have behind them a very long history. It is not without reason that Whitehead noted that philosophy is a series of footnotes to Plato. Footnote is perhaps the wrong word, but it nevertheless emphasises the continuity, and above all, the interrelatedness of the whole of human thought. Artists and philosophers modify, contradict or continue one another, but they do not supersede or replace one another in the way in which the statue and the name of a political deity are replaced by those of the one who ousted him. Sophocles' works and the Gospels are still as valid now, still as ringing with unchallenged truths as when they were written. The scientific discoveries or verifications which have either corrected or disproved some of Pythagoras's or Newton's findings have, far from diminishing, on the contrary increased the stature of their genius, for they have shown both the extraordinary range of their imagination and the oneness of spirit.

The law which Oedipus has broken is the perennial, religious law that man must not make himself a god and that, being born finite, he unavoidably carries with him the limitations of his finitude (some call it sinfulness) which he must accept as he must accept solidarity with his family, his past and the human condition to which he belongs. Irrespective of the causes which led Oedipus to kill his father and marry his mother, he knows that these are sacrilegious deeds for which he must pay; and he can only pay with his own total annihilation. He believes in Divine laws, and he knows that these laws and the Divinity which preside over them, matter more than his individual self; therefore, he knows that he can only restore the integrity of his relations with the Divine by his death which, as a believer, he offers with a special form of exultation. Purely social laws, least of all such utterly contingent notions as the law of social success, cannot be the basis for such compulsions. A man can live, or ought to be able to live, without success, even in a society in which the main value is success, for if he is truly a man, he ought to know that social success is not the kind of value which makes a man, and if he does not know that, he has no moral qualifications for the part of a tragic hero. Willy Loman is both a component member and a victim of a debased society which is a protagonist of the drama in which he is involved. He is himself corrupt from the start, living in illusions, and being part of these illusions, he cannot hope ever to reach a vision of truth which could bring to him the self-awareness of his plight and the redemptory power to save both himself and the society to which he belongs. He therefore dies without illumination, a furtive, uncreative death, wrapped up in illusions and self-pity.

A View from the Bridge is Miller's most original play and his nearest and most successful approach to tragedy. Like so many of his contemporaries, he has turned to the Greek stage for inspiration and he has taken from it two vital ingredients. First a character or hero who, although humble and barely articulate, is led through a kind of incestuous, uncontrollable passion to his unfailing destruction. The forces which compel him to it are as unavoidable as those which compelled Oedipus to his fate. He is not a king or a hero, he is a man afflicted by one of the most elemental and primeval urges which have affected men and which is at the very root of the birth of all the myths about incestuous love and its various punishments. Miller is here on very safe ground as far as motivation of tragic conflicts and destiny are concerned, but the hero lacks grandeur, nobility and self-awareness of his plight, and his melodramatic confrontation with the girl's lover detracts from the noble ritualistic atmosphere of tragedy which lapses for a moment into sensationalism. The second ingredient taken from the Greeks concerns techniques, and it consists in the use of an ever-present lawyer, all knowing, all seeing, who introduces actions, comments upon them and relates them to other similar deeds of the past so as to show the perenniality and universality of certain actions and emotions. He relates the hero to all those compelling figures of the past who, once they had set themselves, or had been set, upon a given course, could not swerve and accepted death as the necessary price of their actions. The plight of Eddie Carbone, led to his death, like a dumb ox, by his incomprehensible incestuous love, is very moving, and although it is nowhere near the terror and pity inspired by the death of more archetypal figures, it is a memorable experience which few contemporary dramatists have been able to convey.

With *After the Fall*, Arthur Miller passes, in spite of his denials, from the subjectivity which characterises *Death of a Salesman* and *The Crucible*, to straightforward autobiography. Although he has taken pains to repudiate such intentions, the shape of this play which is supposed to take place in the memory of a shadowy character called Quentin, is in fact, purely and simply autobiographical. "A rose by any other name would smell as sweet." Whether the hero of Miller's latest offering is called Quentin, Arthur or whatever one likes, his relations with the dramatic character called Maggie, which fill the second act, are undeniably Miller's relations with Marilyn Monroe. And there lies the rub, for no amount of sophistry can transform this obviously lived relationship into an objective, dramatic structure. Maggie is, without a shadow of doubt, Marilyn Monroe and this, more than the other incidents of the play which are also recognisable incidents of Miller's life, is something too naturalistically factual for detached aesthetic appreciation, or for integration in a work of art. Whatever the respective responsibilities of a broken or dissolved partnership, the great shadow of death should dispose of any bitterness or attempts at self-justification and bring only peace to unquiet remains. If the death of a supposedly dear being cannot elicit eulogies like *Lycidas*, *Adonais* or *In Memoriam*, it ought, at least, to elicit silence. Arthur Miller thinks otherwise, and he chooses to use a notorious death for a lesson in psychology, an apologia *pro vita sua* and for public entertainment. Whatever the merits or lack of merits of such an attempt, something which will be discussed presently, its theme and the motives involved, which are, alas, obstrusive enough, are no credit to sensibility or true imagination.

O'Neill masterpiece *The Long Day's Journey Into Night* is, as far as the meaning of the term extends, as autobiographical as *After the Fall*, but with some striking differences. The first one is that O'Neill was a genius. The second is that O'Neill's family was anything but as widely and intimately known as Marilyn Monroe who was the sex idol of her time. O'Neill, in spite of the comparative anonymity of the members of his family, nevertheless did not write his play until the end of his life when the main protagonists of his drama were all dead, and, above all, had died without having become public property. On the contrary, in the case of Miller's play, practically everyone knows Marilyn Monroe's life, her struggles for sanity and her sad end; most people sympathise with her plight, and it is not possible, for the moment, to look upon her as a dramatic character, and not as Marilyn Monroe. This might be possible within twenty or thirty years, but even then, the transmutation will require a greater imagination, a greater faculty of myth-making than seem to be possessed by Arthur Miller who is essentially a naturalistic writer intent upon psychological analyses and social problems. The failure in imaginative transmutation, partly inherent to the nature of the theme and the motives of the main character—Quentin, results in something which is not strictly speaking a play, but an autobiographical story and an attempt at exorcism and psychoanalysis in order to enable the hero to find, at last, happiness. Yet, when all is said and done, the category to which this work belongs is an academic question without much importance. What is important is whether or not this is a work of art, and here it seems to me that, in spite of some remarkable aspects which show the maturation of Miller's dramatic talent and psychological skill, the play is not in the end an organic whole. The two planes of dramatic action which more or less coincide with the division into two acts, do not blend. The first act, devoted to Quentin's relations with his mother, his first wife Louise and his association with un-American activities, achieves, in spite of Quentin's shadowiness, a dramatic objectivity and verisimilitude which pertain to art. The scenes with Louise have a depth of human truth and a psychological acuity which gives them the ring of universality. They are very moving and if not completely dramatic, they abound in affective intensity which rivets attention. The problem is different with the death of Maggie, which is of course unbearably harrowing, but it is not the death of Maggie; it is the death of Marilyn Monroe, and the display of all the wretchedness and abasement of her protracted suicide only serve to emphasise the lack of sensibility which compels an audience to witness it, and unavoidably causes feelings of repellence towards the narrator.

The meeting scene with Maggie is beautifully observed and pervaded with the freshness and simplicity which one associates with some of Marilyn Monroe's impulsive actions. It is her scene; Quentin has not yet assumed the centre of the stage in order to traduce her so as to disculpate himself. He has merely recorded what happened without any attempts to place himself in the best possible light. The result is a scene brimming with innocence and guileless abandon and which make it all the more difficult later, to rid oneself of the notion that whatever Maggie's faults, her basic innocence called for understanding and forgiveness and not for self-righteousness and callousness in order to place upon her the blame for her death. Quentin, who seems to be, above all, concerned with his pride and his urge for self-justification, is a prig and is, in fact, well less-equipped to understand Maggie than was, for instance, Florence to understand Thérèse, in Anouilh's play, *La Sauvage*. He would like to be the knight in armour who rescues her from sin; but he is so conscious of the nobility of his action that he debases Maggie and therefore he can only fill her with bitterness, abjection and a sense of guilt which she did not possess before she met him. He infects her with his obsession with guilt, transposes it on to her so that she may become both scapegoat and the sacrificial victim, and having done that, he presumes, or he hopes, to be found innocent. The fact that he has become retrospectively aware of his lie mildly mitigates his failing, but could hardly absolve him.

QUENTIN: No.

(He suddenly stands and cries out to Listener): Fraud —from the first five minutes! ... Because—I should have agreed she was a joke, a beautiful piece trying to take herself seriously! Why did I lie to her, play this cheap benefactor, this ... What? (Listens, and now, unwillingly): Yes, that's true too; she had; a strange, surprising honor.

He certainly was not aware of it at the time when he was playing at bestowing salvation through the belief that he was taking upon himself the stains of Maggie's past. He has wanted, all along, to be the redeemer.

QUENTIN: When she left, I did a stupid thing. I don't understand it. There are two light fixtures on the wall of my hotel room. (Against his own disgust) I noticed for the first time that they're ... a curious distance apart. And I suddenly saw that if you stood between them—(He spread out his arms)—you could reach out and rest your ...

(Just before he completely spread his arms Maggie sits up; her breathing sounds. He drops his arms, aborting the image. Maggie goes dark.)

Quentin tries many times to spread his arms and to reach the level of Christ, but his longing for altruistic love and innocence have to go through many trials before they reach the appearance of fulfilment with his third wife Holga, who has acquired wisdom and maturity through the searing suffering of concentration camps. She has accepted her guilt, therefore she knows that she is not innocent, and she has reconciled herself with life. So, she hovers over Quentin, ever on the verge of arriving, from the beginning, right to the end of the play.

Before Quentin is fit to be left to her, he obviously has to go through some purifying experiences. He "feels unblessed", he has not been tested by the contact of evil and commitment to goodness. Yet, in fact, how could he? Since to be thoroughly uncommitted under the pretence of innocence seems to be one of his main aims! When his father was dying, he coldly announced to him that his wife had died. When his friend was accused of anti-American activities he let him die without openly taking sides. His father was a kind of Willy Loman—a failure, and Quentin himself has been affected by a sense of failure which enables him to associate with the guilty: "Even in this slaughter-house . . . why does something in this place touch my shoulder like an accomplice? . . . Why is the world so treacherous? Shall one lay it all to the mothers?" He partly does so and says: "here is the final bafflement for me—is it altogether good to be not guilty for what another does?" He obviously believes that it is so, since he tries repeatedly to pass his guilt on to others and to retain an innocence which looks far too much like self-centredness and insensitiveness to those around him. He likes to see himself as a king, blessed by Felice or by Maggie, desired by Elsie, and something completely impervious to the demands of his first wife who could only get his attention when she was required to be used as a listener to test a brief.

The main fault for all this seems to lie with his mother who left him behind, one day when she went to Atlantic City. In the same way, the main cause of Maggie's fear and erratic behaviour seems to rest upon the fact that her mother tried to kill her. Armed with this heavy Freudian and Ibsenian armoury, Quentin marries Maggie in order to save her as he confesses: "from his own contempt". This contempt is present, during most of his relationship with her, and he attempts to save her without being able to fully reconcile himself to her and to give her life. For a brief moment, Maggie has the impression that he really has saved her, and she says so, but this impression is soon dispelled. Indeed, it could not last, for how could anyone who describes truth as "contemptible", know what truth is? Quentin, who declares "I am not innocent, not good", shows clearly that innocence is only a flag which he waves in front of himself, and that he is intent in retaining the appearance of innocence at all costs. The long slow death of Maggie makes clear his insensibility.

> QUENTIN: I'm not counting pills any more, Maggie, I've given up being the policeman. But if you want to, I wish you'd tell me how many you had before I came. 'Cause they should know that in case they have to pump you out tonight. . . .
> QUENTIN: Maggie, I only tell it to you so you'll understand that the question is no longer whether you'll survive, but also whether I will. Because I'm backed up to the edge of the cliff, and I haven't one inch left behind me. And that's the difference tonight, Maggie.

Blind to her plight he obviously is only concerned with himself as when, seeing the unbalanced state she is in, he refuses to take the bottle of pills which she offers him and increases the pressure upon her by telling her that he has talked to the doctor who will soon come to attend to her. This throws her into a panic with the fear of being locked up; meanwhile he continues "Maggie, you want to die and I don't know any more how to prevent it." And Maggie replies "Maybe a little love would prevent it." This sad moving plea gets a dusty answer: "Not that I love you, but if I did, would you know any more? Do you know who I am? Aside from my name? I'm all the evil in the world, aren't I? All the betrayal, the broken hopes, the murderous revenge?"

When she offers the pills once more, he again refuses to take them, and, when she says: "I only wanted to be wonderful so you be proud", Quentin's reply is: "If you could only say, I have been cruel, this frightening room would open! If you could say, I have been kicked around, but I have been just as inexcusably vicious to others; I have called my husband idiot in public, I have been utterly selfish despite my generosity, I have been hurt by a long line of men but I have co-operated with my persecutors. . . ."

> MAGGIE (she has been writhing, furious at this exorcism): Son of a bitch!
> QUENTIN: And I am full of hatred, I, Maggie, the sweet lover of all life—I hate the world!

In the end, he tries to strangle her, and Maggie, exhausted by this fight, the pills and the drinks, dies at last setting him free to walk towards the waiting German bride, who looks as if she was going to be able to match his indifference and self-made innocence. The reader or the listener is left bewildered and gnawed by self-disgust at the awareness that he may well have derived a certain amount of sadistic enjoyment at having been made to watch, as spectacle, the death-throes of an unfortunate human being who should have never been so used for a lesson in psychology and self-justification.

The fiction of the mnemonic psychicodrama no doubt offers great scope to skilful production with impressionistic background, but it is also gimmicky and it militates against any definite dramatic structure in a work which may have had some exorcising value, but about which it is difficult to feel grateful or favourably impressed.

Both Arthur Miller and Tennessee Williams had better look to their laurels, for a new contender who has quite a few assets on his side, has thrown his hat in the ring and already raised strong support. This is Edward Albee, whose last play *Who's afraid of Virginia Woolf?* has been a great success in the United States and has had, on the other hand, a rather mixed critical reception in London. The difference in reaction between the two countries are part and parcel of two rather different attitudes to life and art. The Americans, after a slow start, have now come to revere the intellect and to encourage its growth and development with all the zest of a prosperous society which is becoming more and more conscious of what its debt is to it. The British continue to be distrustful of the intellect and to be rather reserved in encouraging its manifestations when it comes to the arts. With them, the man of feelings, or the dramatic character who bears upon himself the imprint of reality will always win more applause and support than the one who is merely a vehicle for intellectual brilliance.

Who's afraid of Virginia Woolf? is first and foremost a splendid display of intellectual ability. The dialogue is dazzling, the dramatic skill is unflagging and the fertile fancy of the two main characters savaging each other for over three hours, is fascinating and never boring. Its remarkable range is a measure of the intellectual stature of the author, whose versatility, insight in mental violence, viciousness and cruelty is unparalleled on the American stage at this moment. One has to go to Anouilh's *Pauvre Bitos* to find a similar mental savagery. And Anouilh is at his best when savagery is not so much mental as in *Pauvre Bitos*, as deeply rooted in fully rounded human characters, as in *La Valse des Torréadors*, *Le Répétition* or *Ardèle*. Edward Albee's latest play has summoned, in some cases, the name of O'Neill and particularly that of one of his masterpieces, *The Long Day's Journey Into Night*. In both cases we have indeed a quartet of people, yet there is between the two, the fundamental difference which marks a great play from a quite remarkable piece of dramatic writing. The four members of O'Neill's quartet have their feelings, thoughts and reactions, so intrically woven one with the other, that any voluntary or involuntary move by either of them, causes the others to bleed and to ache, while the audience is made to witness a harrowing and illuminating experience. The main reason is that, in spite of the fact that his dramatic characters were so deeply involved with himself, O'Neill's genius nevertheless succeeded in making them heart-rendingly alive and in endowing them with objective reality. They each exist in their own right; they have each their preoccupations and neuroses; they are part of the world around them; they never abstract themselves from it.

In contradistinction with them, George and Martha in Albee's play are practically out of the world, living their own fantasies through the sustained stimulation of drink. The great weakness of Albee's play is that right through it, from beginning to end, one is never really involved with either of the characters, whether in hatred or in sympathy, because these are above all intellectual creations whose savage sport we enjoy, but who are not fully drawn, complete, human beings. The play is a game, an intellectual game, a savage dance, and George calls the last item, the most cruel: "a civilized game", the game which will consist in "getting down to the bone, . . . to get at the marrow", in order to extract the last ounce of suffering and revenge from his love–hate companion—Martha, who says: "Very good, George", when the latter has just finished mauling their two young guests, Nick and Honey, who is quite a compendium of farcical traits. She is capable of hysterical pregnancy, she imbibes brandy non-stop, she throws up like clockwork, and she is so naïvely gullible that she insists that George should make public her weaknesses. The accumulation of incidents, the rather mechanical way in which characters have confessions extracted and then publicised, is perhaps a little too much, so are the mock heroic tone of Martha's speech about the birth and growth of her son, George's accompaniment with excerpts from the mass and his melodramatic announcement of the son's death.

Martha and George seem to be brimful with hatred and violence, yet the fact that George is a failure and that they cannot have children could hardly account for what looks like real madness. The society in which they live, the university campus to which they belong, is of little or no importance; it is merely a ring in which they sport themselves until the last round where they both retire bruised and raw, tired out but not very further away from where they began, except for the fact that Martha seems to be slightly changed, since she confesses that she is now afraid of Virginia Woolf. This makes a very small progression or alteration of character in a play which lacks movement or rather dramatic growth and development, and in which the characters show little gradation of feelings and motivation behind their actions, except that of madness and drink. The play is a series of tableaux or scenes of intellectual fierceness which any one of the characters could terminate much earlier than the final curtain fall, without any serious infringement to logic or to psychological verisimilitude. The fact, for instance, that Nick is an ambitious young man and that Martha is the daughter of the Principal, is a hardly sound enough reason for Nick to allow his wife to be utterly victimised by George. Coleridge's ancient mariner had a mesmerising power, so that the guest had to listen to his story; here on the other hand, one cannot help feeling that there is little reason for Nick and Honey to insist in being battered and bruised and shamelessly embarrassed for more than three hours of sustained, fierce ranting induced by drink and frustration in an entertaining, masterly acted, savage intellectual farce which undeniably displays impressive talent and great hopes for the future of its author. Bearing in mind Tennessee Williams's last plays and silence, and Arthur Miller's doubtful achievement after a rather protracted gestation, one could quite reasonably hail Edward Albee as the new light of the American theatre.

CHAPTER SEVEN

BRECHT

BRECHT, who is one of the three or four major playwrights of the twentieth century, is practically as famous for his dramatic theories and political commitments as for his artistic achievements which often contradict or ignore both. Most artists are a mass of contradictions; Brecht, who is no mean artist, is a bigger mass of contradiction than most. Brecht was politically committed to Marxism and therefore, theoretically at least, his life and writings ought to have been dedicated to the spreading of his beliefs. True political theatre is bound to be like religious theatre, an act of faith and a means of establishing communion among all those who share the same beliefs. Audience and actors are one, and its ideal is that suggested by Stanislavski and explicitly stated by Copeau who said that: "There will be a new theatre only on the day when the man in the auditorium can murmur the words of the man on the stage, at the same time as he and in the same spirit."

Brecht was against identification and against Stanislavski's theories, which, according to him, were part of bourgeois, decadent naturalism. Brecht continually overstates his case, and his artistic theories which might partially be wish-fulfilment, skilful disguises, or excessive rebellion against preceding traditions, are generally toned down and sometimes contradicted by his practice. By the time he began to write, naturalism, which held sway for a brief spell at the end of the nineteenth century, had already been seriously challenged by the revival of poetic drama and poetic productions, by expressionism and by the neo-romanticism of symbolist dramatists. Meyerhold had already rejected Stanislavski's style of production; Copeau and many others had followed in his wake, and the cinema was already beginning to make it clear that there lay the answer to the dream of those who conceived art as a photograph of reality. By the 1920's, expressionism, which flourished best in Germany and central Europe, had expended its strength; therefore, all in all it is quite safe to say that the battle against naturalism and expressionism had already been won before Brecht entered the field.

Brecht's most fundamental belief consists in repudiating the naturalistic illusion that what happens on the stage is real. He is a poet, a man of imagination and he, therefore, starts from the premise that the theatre is illusion, that the audience knows it, and that it must be kept constantly aware of this fact. The rejection of the notion of the theatre as illusional magic and of the theatre as a slice of life, did not of course entail a total rejection of naturalism. This is, in fact, neither possible nor advisable, for both art and life are firmly grounded in the phenomenal world, and no hint of supernatural reality or purely intelligible world is possible without the ground base of phenomenal reality. Brecht knows that all too well and he makes full use of naturalism in his major plays. If the battle against naturalism had already been won, the battle to put an end to the identification of audience and stage characters had never been fought, and in spite of Brecht's efforts, it has neither been won, nor does it offer any prospects of being won, for Brecht himself, in spite of his declared purpose, has been unable to exclude identification from his plays. Even more, these plays, which enable the audience to identify itself, up to a point, with dramatic characters, are indeed his best plays, and they are so because of the very remarkable characterisation which makes it possible for the audience to connect affectively with them. Still, whatever the result, for Brecht, identification of audience with characters on the stage was something positively indecent. His aversion to the emotional involvements of audiences and characters is something pathological and carried to theoretical extremes which were strangely premonitory of the emotionalism and mass hysteria which swept Germany under Hitler's spell. Emotionalism had already had quite a long run in Germany and like Nietzsche, Hölderlin and Goethe, Brecht instinctively longed for Apollonian, calm rationalism as a necessary counterweight to all aspects of intoxications and excesses the Germans are prone to whenever they get carried away by their emotions. Brecht wanted the audience, not to feel, but to think. That is of course a rather tall order which implies both a very specialised audience and a special type of drama which was in fact epic drama as Brecht himself described it and made it famous.

The dramatic action of epic drama, instead of being a complex inter-play of characters and situation, generating suspense, pathos, terror or pity, should be replaced by an objective report of past facts, without any adornments of naturalistic data or attempts at characterisation. The required data are given directly to the audience through announcers, films or writings on boards. Strictly and theoretically speaking, this kind of theatre tends to become either a kind of lecture hall where the audience is instructed and supposedly made to think, or a circus where it is entertained through watching skilful performances. To anyone who might say: "why not send these audiences who wish to be instructed to universities and not to the theatre?" the answer would be that in the theatre the lessons are not given directly but dramatised and illustrated by the performance of actors who interpret and connect the imaginary or historical happenings which they are presenting to the audience. This would be all very well if the aim of the theatre were purely and simply to instruct, and at the beginning of his dramatic career Brecht thought indeed that it should be so. But he soon realised that audiences do not go to the theatre to be instructed, not even Marxist audiences; they want to be entertained; so he had to revert to Molière's well-tried recipe of: "*instruire en amusant.*" "Let us recant", he said in 1948, "from our intentions of emigrating from the realm of the pleasing and let us ... proclaim our intention of settling in this realm. Let us treat the theatre as a place of entertainment. ... But let us enquire about what kind of entertainment we regard as acceptable." This is an unimpeachable statement which could not be improved upon. The pleasure which Brecht regards as acceptable is the pleasure of discovering new truths, something akin to the pleasure of scientific discovery. He wanted the audience to look at dramatic actions in a detached, critical spirit and with the estranged eyes of the discoverers. In order to do that, the audience must be kept constantly on its guard so as not to be carried away by the flow or rhythm of the play or by a possible atmosphere of suspense. In fact, there must not be any suspense or dramatic climaxes which play upon the emotions.

The "epic" play is not an orthodox play, but a succession or a juxtaposition of episodes or scenes which are practically self-contained and make sense by themselves. At the other extreme of Wagner or of Claudel who aimed at total drama by fusing all the various aspects of art—words, music, design, choreography—into oneness, Brecht is intent upon the total autonomy and independence of the various arts which are used as ingredients of the epic theatre. With him, music does not aim at saying what words cannot say or at reinforcing them; on the contrary it either counterpoints them or contradicts them, underlying their falseness. The stage designs do not aim at creating an illusion of reality; they are purely utilitarian, they convey information to the audience which is not goaded into illusion by being suddenly confronted with the lit-up set, but is, on the contrary, invited to inspect and to watch what goes on, with full, unconcealed lights on. Actors or stage hands prepare the stage in full view of the audience in the same way as one lays the table for a meal.

Brecht summed up the difference between what he called the old convention and his own in his usual quirkish, exaggerated ways which never hesitate to give a slight push to truth when truth does not quite move in his direction. He calls the old theatre the "dramatic theatre" as if this were a pejorative term, and he says "The spectator of the dramatic theatre says 'I have felt the same and I am just like this . . . ; this is great art; it bears the mark of the inevitable, I am weeping with those who weep on the stage, laughing with those who laugh.' The spectator of the epic theatre says 'I should have never

thought so; that is not the way to do it; this is most surprising, hardly credible. This human being's suffering moves me
because there would have been a way out for him. This is
great art; nothing here seems inevitable. I am laughing about
those who weep on the stage, weeping about those who
laugh.'" It is hardly worth noting that this piece of jumbled
contradictions and over-simplified antitheses and non-sequi-
turs does not bear serious examination. It can only be taken
as a joke; it is a description of old and new drama about as
accurate as Brecht's interpretation of, or rather distortions
and inventions about, Hamlet. Brecht knew as well as anybody else that only the inmates of an asylum will seriously
identify themselves with any character which takes hold of
their fancy and that no normal member of an audience will
identify himself with Lear, Othello or Phèdre, though of
course, he may, and he generally does, in varying degrees,
share some of their feelings and reactions. The phrase: "This
is great art; nothing here is inevitable" is neither here nor
there. If inevitability precluded great art, some of the
greatest plays the world has known and loved would have to
be struck off the list of great art and be replaced by plays
which embody the Heisenberg principle, which Brecht seems
to advocate as a *sine qua non* for greatness. Brecht ought to
have known better about other contradictions; he ought to
have remembered that the deterministic Marxism in which
he professed to believe could not allow him to entertain
notions like: "by recanting Galileo postponed the dawn of
the age of reason". This is cliché-thinking, and he ought to
have known that Galileo's views had been anticipated and
were shared by others, for neither are ideas ever the monopoly
of a single head nor are human actions a series of disconnected
unpredictabilities. There is coherence even in incoherence,
and human life, at the material as well as at the spiritual
level, is made of interconnected factors which set limits to
unpredictability. Why does Lear decide to submit himself
to a test which is a kind of judgment of God? Nobody can
give a final conclusive answer, possibly not even Shakespeare
himself would have been able to rationalise his fateful

decision. It is something which is part of the very data of the play; it is its starting point in an age where absent gods could no longer be blamed for catastrophes which tested men to the limits of their endurance and raised them from abysses of suffering to heights where they stood on the edge of the Divine which created them. Their tragic fate mediated between man and God, and mediation between finite and infinite is a sacrificial task which calls for the highest qualities which existence can produce. Whatever the causes of Lear's unusual gesture of challenge to Destiny, what follows is as ineluctable as what happens to Oedipus or Agamemnon, and he emerges from his ordeal as heroic a figure as both, and practically as great and as awe-inspiring and moving as the former.

To look at *Lear* in Brechtian terms can only lead to unwarranted distortions of the true nature of the play. A lucid Lear who soliloquises knowingly or criticises his own fateful initial decision would no longer be Lear but a comic character. The same would be true of Macbeth. If instead of being the prey of his ambition and wild imagination, he were to be presented as being a self-critical, calculating, ratiocinating character, he would resemble more a melodramatic criminal than an awe-inspiring, tormented individual in the grip of evil. The intemperate rowdiness of Lear's knights is no historico-social data aimed at building up a politico-social climate or theme; it is merely a small, though necessary, incident in the unfolding of Lear's tragic fate. Whether Goneril was justified or not in dismissing Lear's knights is of no crucial import to the action of the play. She may have been right, yet her subsequent behaviour soon annihilates whatever sympathy one may have granted her on this occasion, and ranges her in the world of the beasts of prey, which, like Edmund, are intent upon gratifying their instincts. Their deceit, lust and amoralism are not part of a Balzacian human comedy, they are part of a world which Lear has to endure and, since his responsibility is involved, redeem through suffering and death. Shakespeare is not after social documents and social justice; he is after trying to render visible and apprehensible some of the mystery of human existence and the strange interdependence of all its aspects. He is after showing that the great winds which shake the earth knock down innocent and guilty alike, for if only the guilty were made to suffer, human life would be as simple as the alphabet and completely circumscribed to the human world and reason. It is the death of innocence which fills the heart with terror and pity and shows both the greatness and the puniness of man; it is the death of innocence, nobly accepted, which transfigures and lifts man above finitude and the boundaries of reason, towards a transcendence which calls him forth.

Without the death of Cordelia which is like a cleansing fire, the play could hardly escape certain melodramatic overtones. Transcending apparent weaknesses of plot and characterisation, Shakespeare's imagination holds together the essential elements of the cosmic struggle between good and evil and welds them into a profound and unique vision of life. The play explodes upon the stage with the abrupt force of a natural phenomenon. No preliminary glimpses of Lear's previous life; no wife for these motherless daughters who will not be themselves mothers; all we have is a sudden, unexpected convergence of Lear's foolishness with his daughters' wickedness for which he himself feels partly responsible. Regan and Goneril are evil through and through; Cordelia is the daughter whom Lear dearly loved, and therefore she only exists as a daughter. She is never allowed to exhibit any other unnecessary aspects of love or behaviour which are not congruent to the play which carries no historico-social details, and ends with the same lack of naturalism with which it began. Its main protagonists are all dead; Kent says that death is not far off, and Edgar's last words, imprint with the same vision, taper off into obscurity and foreboding, like a lamp which, having had its use, quietly splutters out. What matters is the theme—the burning wheel upon which man is pinned and through which earthly evil must have its say. God remains in abeyance throughout, giving free reign to evil, and Lear and Gloucester are only allowed a faint glimmer of joy just before death concludes their harsh unmitigated suffering. Such is life, something which cannot be covered by the term nihilism. Shakespeare's vision of life reaches beyond such lame concepts and posturings in a world which defies understanding. He did not set about to understand; he set about to explore and to reveal the visions of his rational imagination which was not concerned with questions, proofs or condemnations, with theological fears, political hopes or self-generated despair, but with apprehending the birth of life through art.

Whether Lear goes mad out of injured pride and sheer gall at being opposed by his daughter and let down in his judgement and beliefs, or because he is overwhelmed by the cruelty and the chaos which suddenly and unexpectedly confront him, it all boils down to the fact that his reason can no longer comprehend and control the world he has to live in. Whether it was tiredness of responsibilities, onset of mental decay through old age, gerontic petulance or all these things and more inextricably linked together which impelled his first move, they all point to one single conclusion which is that with this move he was taking his first step out of the rational into the irrational world. He was making for the strange, uncharted country which lies between what is and what is not, the mediating country, between finite and infinite, in which telluric forces roam loose and where man must plunge deep down to the roots of despair before he can lift his head and see on the horizon the glowing dawn of salvation. Lear is no Brechtian Galileo tossing and turning between his deep instincts, his fears and his bodily servitudes; he is not living in an historico-social setting which is of primary importance; neither is he consciously repudiating heroism and emotions. He is, on the contrary, made in a heroic mould, and he is overwhelmed by his emotions in a world of chaos and disorder in which human beings have forsaken the natural and rational order, behaving like animals and carrying, as in Breughel's world, animal heads. This is a fragmented, anarchic world from which the values which Lear knew have suddenly disappeared, leaving him utterly bewildered, raging against chaos and seeking refuge in madness.

As one of the key figures of this world which has just col-
lapsed, Lear cannot avoid bearing a great burden of guilt and
responsibility. His sacrilegious gesture in divesting himself of
the crown and of authority has let loose the animality of
Goneril, Regan and others, torn the kingdom apart and
ostracised innocence. Whether one calls it Divine justice, the
laws of nature or purely and simply the dialectics of life, the
fact is that violence calls for violence and death, and crime
and darkness have to be balanced with innocence and light;
for life must go on and hope never completely dies, neither in
blind Gloucester, nor in dying Lear. Whether he crawls about
the ground covered with rags and weeds, or moves, garbed
in regal robes, Lear is a king ever retaining about himself the
aura of supernatural reverence which pertained to kingship.
He is an archetypal, ritualistic figure, crystallising in himself
wide-ranging aspects of human sensibility and enduring a
form of suffering and death which is both particular and
universal. Being a creation of genius, on a grand scale, he is
a concentration of spirit embracing wide and profound
aspects of human life which transcend time and history. His
plight is partly individual, partly a ritualistic re-enactment of
the most crucial aspect of the human condition which implies
errors and fall and redemption through suffering. He is a
mediatory hero in the wake of Oedipus, Socrates, Buddha
and Christ.

King Lear is not, like most of Brecht's plays, a polemical,
wilfully educational play, it is creative experience to be
absorbed through imagination, and to grant undue importance, least of all, pre-eminence to social considerations in
tragic plays, is to scale them down to the level of documentary evidence for historico-social moments, while tragedy
reaches beyond such moments, into timelessness. Brecht has
made it perfectly clear that tragedy and epic drama were at
opposite poles, and his own wide artistic range shows that
there are various roads to truth, and that they do not all pass
through historicism, socialisation and Verfremdungseffekt.

The more one reads Brecht's critical writings and eccen-
tricities, the more one realises that they should be taken with
fistfuls of salt. "The actor," he says, "should not impersonate a

character; he should simply narrate the actions of this character and represent the appearances of the character whose actions he is both narrating and commenting upon." Now, this is certainly no novelty from whatever angle one looks at it. Shakespeare's soliloquies and asides to the audience, in *Richard III* for instance, are nothing but comments of the actor on his own behaviour, and in *A Midsummer Night's Dream* he showed that he knew everything from A to Z about alienation. The *Pyramus and Thisbe* players are rehearsed and made to perform according to rules which make it look as if they, and not Brecht, had written the *Little Organon for the Theatre*. The actor who is going to play the lion reassures the audience that he is no lion; the one who plays the wall uses his two hands to represent the chinks through which the lovers converse. In fact, everything in this little play within the play is a piece of let-us-pretend, with feelings enacted and not lived, and with the obvious conclusion that what takes place on the stage is not reality, but a game. The theatre has never been a church (except for religious plays), but a house of illusions in which people come to watch a game and to play the game of watching it as a let-us-pretend game. How could it have been otherwise in Shakespearian days with all the comings and goings which went on while the play was enacted and when productions carried no naturalistic scenery? How could it have been otherwise in the age of Louis XIV, when the stage was crowded with toshed-up "marquis" and titled people sitting there to be seen and to look around, and certainly not to add to the verisimilitude of the play? The debate about identification of actor and character is old, very old. Diderot set it out in memorable terms and the French, long before Brecht, have always talked about *"composer un rôle"*. No actor in his senses can think that he is the character that he is impersonating. If he did so, his own place would be in an asylum, and not on the stage where he could not harmonise his performance with that of his fellow performers. He can only do so through constant watchfulness and judgment. The cellist Paul Tortellier put this point admirably when, talking to one of his pupils, he said "you must never be carried away by your performance, you must both perform and listen to yourself performing, not as yourself but as if you were a member of the audience. That is the way to be critical and without indulgence for oneself."

Claudel's *Christoph Colomb* which was written in 1927, published in 1929 and produced by the Berlin State Opera in 1931, shows plenty of examples of alienation and devices which were later used by Brecht and Brechtians. There are film sequences, there is an announcer, there are subtitles, and there is a running criticism of the play by the members of the stage audience. It's all done there before Brecht came on the scene. Before Claudel or Brecht, Anatole France, in his short story *Crainquebille,* had used quite a few Brechtian recipes. This is not meant as a bad mark for Brecht, but simply in order to show that, at times, he propounded, with great seriousness, truths which had by then already become fully-fledged artistic practices. That Brecht should advise actors to control their emotions and to avoid the excessive ranting which mars the playing of heavy parts, is something reasonable and readily understood, particularly in connection with the German theatre. But ranting is merely bad acting. Hamlet had already made the point in his advice to his players; a good actor can convey greater intensity by his silences than by vocal or muscular displays. Brecht was against any form of emotionalism; he wanted every form of feeling to be thoroughly sifted and processed through the mind. This is indeed a very legitimate approach for the type of drama which he practised with success and which is epic drama, but it is obvious that one cannot reduce all aspects of drama to this formula. It is the same about acting. "The actor", says Brecht, "must act in such a manner that one might see alternative courses of action . . . so that any given action is only one among a number of variants." Again, that can only be true of certain types of actions which are of course Brecht's predilections and the basis of his theatre. Galileo can make clear his hesitations and the alternatives he could have adopted, because he is in many ways, like his creator, shifty and wily, and because he is what Montaigne would have described as: *"ondoyant et divers"*, adapting himself to circumstances and using his mind to feed his belly, to improve his lot or to foster his ambitions. He reflects Brecht's wisdom when he said: "The only way to deal with authority is to outlive it." But this kind of intellectual approach to dramatic creation and acting cannot be valid with characters who are, rightly or wrongly, possessed with strong ideals or passions, and in whom reason has ceased to be allowed to weigh the pros and cons and has been swamped or swept aside by the affective or idealistic flood. Of course, these are typically non-Marxist attitudes which Brecht condemns, forgetting the fact that, without the passionate idealism of the pre-revolutionary Bolshevists, the Tsar would still be ruling over Russia and *Das Kapital* would be a dust-laden library curiosity, and not the basis of world-ranging institutions. Besides that, if Galileo fits Brecht's precepts, *Mother Courage* does not. Whatever the causes—circumstantial, social or personal—of her single-mindedness, she goes on and on, through sorrows and death, carrying on her inhuman trade in an inhuman world, and it is obvious that nothing will stop her except fatal illness and death. She is neither a good Marxist nor a good Brechtian and a thoroughly alienated character. The audience cannot help being partial to her toughness and forgiving to her amoralism, even although it knows that it should not do so. She fails to conform to the Marxist rules, and she is, of course, what she should not be in epic drama—a great character.

To Brecht, what matters, at least in theory, is not the characters and their feelings but the story in which they are involved, and the way they behave towards one another. Yet, of course, gestures and actions imply feelings and emotions, and the emphasis upon gesture and action leads straight to Barrault, to Marcel Marceau and to those who strongly believe in mimed, stylised, and even in danced actions. The search for an appropriate action or gesture leads to the decomposition of the play into the main elements of the story or fable which holds it together, and if possible, to embodying each of these elements in one single basic action, attitude, or gesture, an incident which impresses itself upon the audience. The actors are grouped or are directed to move and to act so as to express these basic actions or attitudes with the maximum economy and elegance. "The stage," says Brecht, "does not reflect the natural disorder of things, ... it aims at the natural order of things, and the point of view to achieve this order is historical and sociological." The links between the various parts of the actions have, according to him, to be clearly stressed so as to give the audience plenty of time to think, irrespective of Priestley's assertion, "that nobody goes to the theatre in order to think". Brecht was certainly obsessed with thinking, rationality and elegance. These were his Apollonian dreams, the wish-fulfilment of the German psyche trying to keep at bay its dark tides and its emotionalism. His motto seemed to be: "Let it be light, light is everything." For him no murkiness, no conjurers' tricks; the stage had to be fully lit up, and light was used, not to create mood or atmosphere, *pace* Gordon Craig, but so that everybody could see clearly what was going on. The musicians were not buried in the bowels of the proscenium but placed on the stage, so that music could have its adequate say against the words. Songs are used as interludes which give the audience time to recover its wits and to reflect, and their titles or subject matter were either announced by a blare of trumpets so as to awaken everyone, or by flags hanging from flies. The actors were given no chance to identify themselves with their parts, and in order to prevent that, Brecht used the cunning device during rehearsals of incorporating the stage directions in the spoken text of the actors. This kind of practice turned drama into a narrated epic or a chronicle reporting of past deeds and precluded any attempt at living them on the stage.

Brecht's obsession with emotions in art and acting and with separating the audience from the happenings on the stage is neither new nor singular to him. Diderot, in *Le Paradoxe du Comédien*, had dealt exhaustively with the problem of emotions and their representation on the stage. "Les larmes du comédien", he had said, "descendent de son cerveau; celles de l'homme sensible montent de son cœur; ce sont les entrailles qui troublent sans mesure la tête de l'homme sensible; c'est la tête du comédien qui porte parfois un trouble passager dans les entrailles; il pleure comme un prêtre incredule qui prêche la Passion; comme un séducteur aux genoux d'une femme qu'il n'aime pas, mais qu'il veut tromper, comme un gueux dans la rue ou à la porte d'une église qui vous injurie, lorsquil désespère de vous toucher, ou comme une courtisane qui ne sent rien, mais qui se pâme entre vos bras". Eliot, in our time, has said that art is not a turning loose of emotions but on the contrary a flight from emotions. Although, of course, to fly from emotions, one must first have emotions. Brecht, who obviously knew all about emotions, denied towards the end of his life that he wanted to banish emotions from the stage: "The epic theatre", he said, "in no way renounces emotions, least of all emotions like love of justice, the urge to freedom and justified anger . . . it tries, in fact, to strengthen them and to evoke them. The critical attitude into which it is trying to put its public cannot be passionate enough."

Brecht obviously equated naturalism, which he disliked, with the emotional involvement of audiences with dramatic characters. He failed to realise that no amount of intellectual gymnastics will enable one man to grasp something of another man's experience, unless there is a certain amount of emotional identification or repulsion between the two. Imagination is not like the intellect, confined to abstractions; yet it is the only possible source of artistic experience and of true reality. Brecht believed that what he called (God knows why) the non-Aristotelian epic theatre was destined to become the theatre of the scientific age. He saw in it the typical Marxist theatre and an instrument of social change. He nursed the strange notion that by turning audiences into critics and preventing them from looking at dramatic conflicts through the dramatic characters' point of view, the audience would discover the Marxist solution to the problems in which the characters were involved. An audience of trained Marxists might, and would in all likelihood do that, but any other audience can only attempt to solve the dramatic conflict which it witnesses according to the data which it is offered. If this type of data is part of the play, then it is no longer a play but a piece of propaganda, and Brecht the playwright and poet could not allow Brecht the Marxist to use plays for propaganda. He would very much have liked to have it both ways, but he was too good an artist to confuse art with Marxism; the result was that he found it very difficult to please the Marxists and that his plays had a much greater success in the capitalist West than on the Eastern side of the iron curtain. Whatever one might say about him, his life and work show that he was first and foremost an artist and not a man of strong political or moral convictions. His theatre is more a theatre of doubt than of proselytism. He attacks cant and conventions, he asks questions and indeed sends the audience in desperate search for answers and solutions, as is the case with his master play, *Galileo*, but he himself does not offer solutions. He believes that an audience faced with the contradictions of society would necessarily turn towards Marxism; but this is, of course, only a pious hope not verified by experience. Why indeed should an audience, witnessing the havoc played by war in *Mother Courage*, turn to Marxism? This spectacle would most certainly strengthen pacifist feelings, but there is no reason in it which could turn the audience towards a Marxist solution; for there we see the representative of the proletariat—Mother Courage—battening on war, whatever the cost, and merely adding evil to evil in a play which is moving and which makes facts speak with utmost poignancy. On the other hand, the stark confrontation of Mother Courage with her son's dead body stabs the heart with the utter wretchedness of the human condition, and is a moment packed with emotion and worthy of ancient tragedy.

Brecht, of course (a well-meaning Marxist), repudiated the notion of tragedy. Despair is indeed a capital sin in Marxist theology; optimism must always prevail. The world may be ploughing through fire and catastrophes, but according to Marxism, it moves towards justice and the ideal society. Capitalism is doomed, and we all know it is, for anything human is indeed doomed to change and to be replaced by something else; but the point is, will this something else be

Marxism? Only the Marxists believe that it will be so, and thus we are straight into tautological thinking or, better, in the world of beliefs. Brecht believed, like all Marxists, in the dialectical process of history, but he was, as a poet, a man of "negative capabilities" and a kind of anarchist who did not enjoy party discipline. Like everyone else, he found it difficult to rationalise Marxism's inherent contradictions, the main one being that which lies between its determinism and its final optimism. This optimism is the only thing which differentiates it from Greek necessity and from the very basis of Greek tragedy, which, if not optimistic in existential terms, was given a redemptory end. If, according to Marxism, all is well in the end, suffering and catastrophes are merely gratuitous happenings which only serve to show human heroism and endurance and are therefore a source of pathos and admiration. Such is the case with *Mother Courage*. Her way of making a living is undeniably immoral, yet her resilience and indomitable courage are a tonic to the human heart which cannot but respond with sympathy, unmindful of Brecht, who did not want that. He wanted the audience to draw its own conclusions which should be such as to aim at overthrowing the existing rotten, social order. The Communist Party, on the other hand, did not want the audience to be left in doubt as to what to do. It wanted it to be explicitly told what to do, for according to the Communist faith, any work of art, play or novel which does not tell the reader or audience what to do, lacks social context and is merely guilty of formalism. Naturalism, which presents things as the senses apprehended them, is just as bad. The only form of art that the party can countenance is social realism which ascribes to art the function of presenting a picture of society as it ought to be or will soon be in a socialist state. This is, in fact, art as wishful thinking or medication for mentally deficient people who cannot face reality. The medicament must not only be for a specific end; it must also be sweet, and easy to swallow. In other terms, the audience, as far as plays are concerned, must see clearly where it is going and be given very simple material. Brecht was the opposite of simple. He was, on the contrary, sophisticated, ambiguous, indirect and never explicit. He was therefore deviating from the party line and he was very often told about it, yet in vain; he went on his own sweet, poetic way. Although he constantly refused to tell audiences where to go, he certainly knew where he himself was going. He was not going to worship Stanislavski's method; he was against it. He was, in fact, on the side of Stanislavski's former friend and collaborator, Meyerhold, who had anticipated Brecht by insisting that actors should never forget that they are acting, and that they should do so in a style shorn of emotionalism, and imprint with "epic" calm and coolness. Meyerhold, condemned as a formalist, spent his life in exile out of Russia.

Brecht was neither a Soviet nor an East German citizen, so he could not be exiled. But the main point was that, although he failed to be a social realist he was a useful means of propaganda for the West; so, his theatre was generously supported and encouraged by East German officialdom, even although he never won full assent and acclaim in the Soviet Union. How could he? His use of masks and his transmutations of reality were condemned as formalism, and his stark representation of reality received the objectionable label of naturalism. Even *The Mother*, his most didactic play, did not pass muster in Russia which labelled it formalist. *Mother Courage* and *Lucullus* were rejected as pacifist plays; *The Caucasian Chalk Circle*, which preaches that things should be given to those who make best use of them, could hardly be a great success in Russia. As for *Galileo* and his plea for the freedom of scientific enquiry, it was bound to have as much chance of success in Russia as his early nihilistic plays.

Brecht's Marxism failed to please the Marxists and was a source of suspicion for the West which distrusted this aspect of his work and personality and applauded what he was trying to ban from his plays—emotions. Not only was he a typical illustration of the morality of La Fontaine's famous fable *Le Meunier, son fils et l'âne*, which is that: *"on ne peut pas contenter tout le monde et son père"*, but he was also caught in the cleavage which always exists between intentions and final results and effects. He wanted to eliminate emotions, and his works constantly belie his aims. *Mother Courage* is obviously a kind of morality play meant as a warning against the dangers and the stupidity of profiteering from war. The result is quite different; through scenes of precise, matter of fact, unsentimental exactitude, the play shows how Mother Courage is slowly deprived of all she cared for and is left drained of sorrows and shorn of everything except her indomitable, moving courage. Brecht rewrote the play so as to make clear the villainy of the woman; it was of no avail; she apparently still remains an example of unbreakable resilience and of the harsh fate of the downtrodden poor who are ever victims of society's greed and wars and can do nothing but grin and bear it. Another conclusion which emerges with this play is that all soldiers are beasts. Galileo, who was intended as a villain, was hailed by several critics as a hero of science.

With *The Measure*, Brecht had intended to write an apology for party discipline; yet, one of the four party members fails to follow the party orders and his compassion for Chinese coolies leads to his death at the hands of his comrades whom the party absolves of their guilt. Like Sartre's *Les Mains Sales*, it shows that party discipline cannot always counter human emotions. The result is that this play, which was intended to boost the Communist faith, is banned in Communist countries. This paradoxical result makes it clear that an artist's commitment to a party or a cause does not mean that such an artist will only produce works faithful to the party or the cause he has espoused. His subconscious may pull him in a direction quite different from that of his rational commitments. Above all, his artistic imagination and creativeness will, if he is a true artist, assume control of whatever he is trying to do and will do it, not in order to meet the requirements of a political creed, but those of the inner laws of artistic creation. A committed artist may wilfully choose certain subject-matters or themes in which he may see possibilities of combining both his inner affinities with them and his rational commitment to them. But he soon realises that it is always the inner affinities and correspondences which matter, and not the rational, wilful choices made in the name of extra-artistic reasons. Any artist intent on discovering the truths which correspond to his true being cannot but end in rejecting any form of restriction on the full range of his vision and inner integrity. Any form of commitment to a narrow ideology or creed, and political creeds are always both narrow and extremely relative, cannot but inhibit a true creative genius, who, however much he may deplore his incapacity to serve his political party through art, will have to confine his support of that party to his actions and behaviour as a man. Even commitments to a transcendental faith like the Christian, could, in certain cases, cause conflicts between artistic necessities and the tenets of that faith.

Brecht knew very well the power of the forces of the subconscious, but had not always been a self-confessed rationalist and classicist. The beginning of his life shows him to be in a Lawrencian mood, much entranced with the dark forces of nature and of the subconscious. Baal, the hero of his first play, quite reminiscent of Claudel's *Tête d'or*, is a typically romantic, satanic hero who obviously has the admiration of the author. The next four plays show that Brecht is still entertaining the same beliefs. Whether in the jungle of Chicago, where two men are locked in a love–hate struggle, in *Edward II* or in *Man is Man*, one finds the same nihilism and the same belief that man is merely a plaything of nature, unable to understand and to communicate with his fellow-beings or to control his environment. All the characters of these early plays, some of them homosexual, are tossed about by the inner compulsions of a nightmarish world and are totally isolated one from the other. This is what one might call Brecht's dark, nihilistic phase, something which helps one to understand his insistence upon rationalism and upon mastery of the emotions. The political faith which he embraced helped him to break away from nihilism by giving him an aim and by compelling him to submit his thoughts and behaviour to the approval of reason and to his chosen vocation; in fact, the two went together, for Marxism's main claim is its scientific rationality. This is Brecht's didactic phase, and the conflict between emotions and rationality is one of the main themes of his dramatic work. In *The Exception is the Rule,* the coolie who tries to help his master becomes a victim of his good intentions. *The Rise and Fall of the City of Mahagonny* shows that the gratification of instincts leads to destruction and irrational impulses can only be subdued by violence.

The Communists believed that violence was the only way to bring about the destruction of capitalism. Brecht shows his customary caution by not taking sides on this delicate point. He confines himself to showing violence in action. The conflict between reason and emotions was still unresolved, so Brecht, who knew better than most how to have his cake and to eat it, indulged feelings and lyrical exuberance but criticised and tempered them with directness of expression and irony. Irony is the master key to ambivalence. With irony one can juggle with feelings and, at the same time, annihilate them, and if a dramatic character can both show his feelings and his irrationality, and yet criticise them, he can indulge the full range of human affectivity without risk of succumbing to any aspect of it and, above all, without incurring criticism. Dialectics enabled Brecht to rationalise his conflicts, while the ultimate triumph of Marxism could only endow him with the optimistic belief that in the end justice would prevail. These are the kind of beliefs which colour the rich, complex plays of his last phase. In these plays, the characters are allowed a greater range of emotions and humanity; and of course, the more human a character is, the more inevitable the process of identification with the audience is. Mother Courage, Grusha, Azdak, the Mother are such characters. Mothers are among the most moving of Brecht's feminine characters, who are generally prostitutes, infanticides or foster mothers like Grusha and Shente. Grusha is a better mother than the true mother; she rightly gets the custody of the child and the full sympathy of the audience. Neither she, nor her fiancé, nor the judge Azdak, who are the three most human characters of the *Chalk Circle*, wears a mask. Grusha and Azdak are perfectly characterised, in fact, the latter is perhaps the best-drawn of all Brecht's characters;

he is quite worthy of being placed in the Shakespearian gallery as the model of a likeable rogue. Grusha is both moving and intellectually interesting, and she makes it perfectly clear that violence cannot be a means of achieving goodness. The emotions which she shows are generous and altruistic, and Brecht has, with masterly skill, integrated them in a play which is a complex dramatic entertainment, one of his best plays, and certainly one of the major plays of our time.

Galileo, Brecht's master play, shows the same repudiation of violence and the same complex integration of various aspects of the emotional life; he is both one of the greatest scientists of all times, and a man governed by his instincts. His urge to go on with his researches is his basic instinct— the expression of his essential self, which nothing but death can alter. In order to gratify this essential self, he is prepared to do anything—to lie, to cheat, to grovel and to indulge in low deeds. He is even prepared to recant so as to gain time and to finish his work. His reply to his disciple's cry: "Pity the country that has no heroes", is: "Pity the country that needs heroes!" Years later, when the same disciple visits him for the last time before going to Holland, he hands him the manuscript which his recantation has enabled him to complete. His disciple, thinking that he understands at last the motive of his recantation, hails him as a hero, but Galileo, who knew clearly what he meant when he deplored the fact that countries should require heroes, refuses his disciple's praise, for he can already anticipate the terrible import of his action. He sees himself as a criminal who has opened the way to science, being as much a tool of the state as the Pope is shown to be a tool of the institution of which he is head.

Galileo knows that he cannot be a hero for he depends too much on the pleasures of the senses. The author of *Misery and Grandeur of the Third Reich* had seen through the hollowness of heroics, and his great creations like Galileo, Mother Courage or Azdak are as riddled with contradictions as he himself and his nation were. His nation had been brought low by violence, and part of it perhaps still dreamt of regaining, through violence, what violence had lost. She had been the prey of emotions which might once again erupt and defy rationality. Brecht was very conscious of these conflicts and he sought to resolve them through his professed adherence to Marxist doctrine. He did not, he could not succeed, and his plays are in some ways the outcome of the centrifugal forces which were in him. Wily and cautious though he was in life, he faced his artistic problems with uncompromising honesty and realism which could not be hoodwinked by any political creed. He had no illusions about rich or poor, capitalists or proletarians. He felt that if the poor became rich they would be just as bad as the rich. His world is like Sartre's or Anouilh's, a ruthless world in which innocence is soon corrupted and justice and love have no place. "Next to you", he said in *The Exception is the Rule*, "someone is thirsty; quickly close your eyes! Plug up your ears, someone is groaning next to you! Retract your foot; someone is calling for help." The Marxism in which he believed could never lure him into singing the joys of the promised land. He hoped that such a dream might one day come to be realised, but the present reality was far too harsh to enable him to indulge in dreams. Society was corrupt and as ruthless as any ancient fate, yet society is made up of men who must bear the blame of their social meanness and corruption. And if men are so, what grace or force can change them? Grace! The Communists don't believe in it. Force! Some do and some don't. Brecht did not, for he knew that violence degrades anyone who uses it; so he could not write the type of plays which Marxists would have liked him to write. They had to make do, not with his message, but with his dramatic fame and with the fact that he shared their political beliefs. But his major plays which place him in the forefront of twentieth-century drama, are profoundly human and permeated with the contradictions and the wisdom of his very complex nature which was that of an important poet and a major dramatist.

Brecht's theories have been used and misused by skilful imitators who thought that they could pass themselves as lions by wearing this animal's skin. Unfortunately an ear or a foot always breaks through and makes it clear that the roar is fake. Brecht, the most influential playwright of his time can certainly be imitated by writers and producers, or used as a yard-stick by critics, but a little Brechtian flavouring goes a long way, and overdoses of it easily turn to parodies. His complexities were essentially his own; his nature was ambivalent or, even more, polivalent and dialectical. Nothing for him was what it looked. Even Demons found it very hard to be angry, while Goodness itself could only wear a distorted mask:

> A wooden Japanese mask hangs on my wall
> The swollen veins in the forehead showing
> What a strenuous business it is to be angry.

Brecht knew what a strenuous business it was to be a political propagandist or to look upon human beings as the tools of a wilful dialecticism. In genius, the human heart must needs have its say, and Brecht was a genius; so his great characters generally walk out of the classroom where they are sometimes supposed to stay, on to the road of living and suffering, and they struggle with the problems which confront them, in a concrete and singular way which makes them and their author, memorable. Like Yeats, Brecht made himself a coat of many colours but he truly soared when he started from the "foul rag and bone of the heart".

CHAPTER EIGHT

GERMAN-SPEAKING DRAMATISTS
AFTER BRECHT

I

Two German-Speaking Swiss

Brecht's mantle lies now on the ground; nobody could wear it, yet the German voice is not silent. There are two German-writing Swiss—Friederich Dürrenmat and Max Frisch, and a German—Rolf Hochhuth, who are already rising towards world fame. Though at this stage, it is not possible to undertake an exhaustive assessment of their work, one could not, at the same time, omit their names from a conspectus of contemporary drama. While quite a few of Dürrenmat's plays have already been performed in this country, Max Frisch's work has not been so widely staged. One is therefore compelled to rely, in his case a good deal, on the published text. Though it is widely held that, as far as plays are concerned, the stage is the thing, the written text of these plays together with *Andorra*, which has been recently produced in London, leave little doubt as to Max Frisch's present stature. *The Fire Raisers* is a brilliantly inventive, and topical "morality play". As for *Andorra*, no contemporary playwright since Brecht has succeeded, as Frisch has succeeded in this play, in raising a topical, wide-ranging issue like that of anti-semitism, to the level of a fully integrated complex of human beings, involved in a kind of archetypal conflict which pertains to twentieth-century social life. Avoiding hollow expressionism and shadowy allegory, the setting is convincingly drawn and the characters have the hallmark of types which could be Andorrans as well as whatever other nationality one could think of. The plight of the cowed schoolmaster, that of his ex-mistress, that of his sacrificial daughter and above all, that of his son Andri who assumes his fate in a way similar to that with which Christ assumed his regal crown of thorns, is the kind of moving and chastening experience which one encounters in tragedy.

Andri is painfully led through the various stations of his calvary and rejections, until the moment when he is told the truth, at last, it is too late. This truth looks too much like all the untruths that he has been previously offered. The mechanism of the plot is admittedly rather creaky and it is bound to be deemed even more so, if the play is looked upon as some kind of partly naturalistic drama and not as a symbolic representation of a given aspect of social life. Even so, it is difficult not to notice the protracted unwillingness of the father to confess the truth to his son, to say nothing of the perfunctory and totally unconvincing way in which the Priest attempts to reveal this truth. Judged by the stern laws of naturalism, the play would be found wanting; but to attempt to do so would be just as bad as looking for the birth certificate of Hamlet or for the marriage lines of Lady Macbeth. The Brechtian formula of anonymous characters like the carpenter, the innkeeper, the journeyman, etc., who, every now and then step out of the present of the dramatic action and explain their behaviour to the audience as if they were in a courtroom, make it clear from the start that this is a Brechtian play and not a naturalistic or a stricly speaking dramatic play. The mechanical aspect of the characters and their generic names clearly indicate that they do not really matter as individuals; they only matter as the component parts of an imaginative picture. The lack of speech differentiation stresses the anonymousness and the interchangeability of the corrupt component elements of the society within which the play takes place. Finally, one must add to these facts the lack of emotional texture which renders indentification between audience and characters practically impossible.

The play is above all, a parable about the baseness, cruelty, conformism, and guilt-feelings which are part of modern society. The climate of the play is that of the last war, with

the Blacks—the locusts, the anti-semites, representing the
Nazis. The anti-semitism of the Nazis is supported by the
racialism of Andorrans like the carpenter who says to Andri:
"Everyone should do what he has in his blood . . . you can
earn money."* The Andorrans are smug, self-satisfied
neutralists, riddled with self-guilt and intent upon throwing
all the responsibility for their failings on some victim or out-
cast whose blood will pay for their sins. To complete the
atmosphere of the last war, there is even the shaving of the
young woman's head as a means of punishment and shame
as was the case with the women of occupied countries who
fraternised or collaborated with the enemy. The play is both
topical and perennial, particular and general. Therefore it is
not the physical or moral taking on of Jewishness which so
much matters, as the fact that Andri is turned into a Jew by
anti-Jewish fellow-beings who need a scapegoat for their lies,
egoism and turpitudes, Andri's father is a deceitful coward;
his sister gives in to lust and betrays him; the priest is a supine
character who can only lift his eyes to heaven, wash his hands
of other people's guilt, and pray. As for the two mothers, they
are, in spite of the hauntingly brief appearance of Andri's
mother who dies as a victim, too shadowy to counteract the
rot of the society in which Andri lives and to prevent his
destruction. It is not the illusion of Jewishness which prevents
him from believing the priest; it is the fact that the betrayals,
lies and inhumanity which he has endured have killed his
capacity to hope and to believe in the future, and in the alien
society to which he belongs; therefore, the only thing that
remains for him to do is to die.

In as far as this play is Brechtian, it is a spectacle depicting
a social structure and its effects, upon some of the individuals
which compose it, but without any attempt at psychological
depths or sustained verisimilitude. Some of the characters are
simply used as appearances of social manifestations exhibited
on the stage, and the acting must needs partake of this surface
presentation of the characters, which is a kind of pure
phenomenalism without any involvement or identification

* *Three Plays by M. Frisch*, p. 185. London, 1962.

with them, even in the case of the key character of Andri who is progressively transformed by what happens to him and who shows this transformation by his refusal to trust anyone. He exhibits one aspect of Jewishness which rises far beyond the unimportant problem of the historicity of the Jewishness of Christ, and which reaches the perennial, and it is the aspect of the scapegoat, or of the chosen sufferer for other people's sins. He is therefore not specifically a character but a sign or a symbol for a complex of feelings and attitudes brought about by society. Christ's redemptory mission is as social as any thorough-going Marxist could possible make it. It is not man alone (an unthinkable notion) but social man which is sinful, and in this respect Marxist and Brechtian views co-incide with Christianity. Society made of Andri who accepts it, a victim, in the same way as, according to Sartre, it made of Genet who accepted it also—a thief. Andri, who is quite a Brechtian character, reveals or makes clear to the audience, the effect of lies and hatred upon an individual, but does not call forth sympathy or identification, because the structure and climate of the play, with all the devices which the author has used, preclude such an identification. The spectator is not asked to take sides as when confronted with the crude emotionalism of *The Representative*; he is asked, or rather to be more precise, he is orientated by the structure of this kind of Brechtian play towards assessing, through his own consciousness, the interplay of individual and social forces, so as to derive from it enlightenment and an incentive to action. All in all, *Andorra* seems to me one of the important plays of our time and certainly a remarkable achievement.

Compared with it, and the comparison is unavoidable, since the goal is similar, *The Physicist*, by Dürrenmat is definitely contrived, mechanical and melodramatic. The charade of the madmen who claim to be world-famed scien-tists and who are apparently compulsive stranglers of their nurses, is suddenly turned into a merry-go-round of inter-national spies and a supposedly Promethean genius who, afraid that the secret which he has stolen from the gods might be used to set the world ablaze, tries to hide under the cloak of madness which nevertheless involves him in the evil of murder. The didacticism and the *deus ex machina* solution of the mad doctor who has seen through the ploys and disguises of the spies and the scientist and holds them all, and the rest of the world, in his power, might be worthy of a circus performance in which the master acrobat tops the pyramid; it draws indeed a gasp of amazement; but it certainly leaves the head cool and the heart unruffled. *The Visit* is a better play; it is a masterly demonstration of the power of money and of Dürrenmat's inventiveness, fantasy, stark realism, sense of macabre and highly polished language. These are the ingredients of a quite original dramatic talent, and the comments made here should only be taken as an all too brief introduction and tribute to the work of two remarkably adult writers, and as an expression of the belief that both Frisch and Dürrenmat are already notable landmarks of the contemporary theatre and can only increase their stature.

II

ROLF HOCHHUTH

The Representative is for the moment Rolf Hochhuth's only play, and, like Miller's last play, it has left behind it a trail of acrimony and heated arguments for the very important reason that the matter used, that is to say, the content of these two plays has not been transmuted into an organic and fully integrated artefact, something which precludes any other arguments, except those which are concerned with the aesthetic worth of the play. The events used in these two plays are far too recent and above all, too well known by millions to make acceptable imaginative transmutations (even if imagination had been truly at work) which have strayed too far from widely known reality. The dramatist is admittedly neither an historian nor a psychologist recording a straightforward clinical case, yet, whether he deals with historical characters or with psychological cases, these must be remote enough from his time or from his personal emotions to enable him to avoid using his characters as mouthpieces for his feelings and ideas or as material for the dramatisation of the thesis he has set himself. John Osborne has, up to a point, found in the character of Luther an objective correlative for his own rebelliousness and anger against social ills. Yet, he is nowhere damagingly unfaithful to the historical character of Luther, and although he treats the Pope with the superciliousness and the gay abandonment of one who may have been used to singing "Tuz lurn, kick the Pope", he merely overstresses, in relation to the general balance of the play, a minor and over-emphasised aspect of the effete behaviour of certain popes. This picture, slanted though it is, does not obtrusively jut out of the aesthetic canvas, and, therefore, it is, up to a point, justified, and accepted as part of a dramatic work and not as part of a slice of life, something which would call for a non-aesthetic response.

Such is not the case with *The Representative*, a play in which the feelings generated by the text are in some cases too obviously those of the author and not those of dramatic characters whose conflict should produce great drama. To regret or to deplore the fact that the Pope choose to avoid condemning, openly and in clear-cut terms, the destruction of the Jews by Hitler is a matter of opinion rationally held, and of sadness widely and genuinely felt by many fervent Catholics like François Mauriac, eminent churchmen like Cardinal Tisserand, and by others who believe that the Vicar of Christ ought to have thrown himself, uncompromisingly, on the side of the Martyrs. Irrespective of the great help which the Vatican and numerous church prelates and monastic orders gave to the persecuted Jews, one is quite entitled to think that a call from the Pope to resist such inhuman cruelties, even at the cost of large-scale martyrdom for the Catholic Church, would have been a more heroic and more fecundating gesture for the Church than that of a rationally justified caution. But these can only be opinions. It is obviously difficult to be dogmatic on this point, for the import of a declaration of large-scale defiance could not have been anticipated. Although hindsight might incline us, or some of us, towards an uncompromising attitude, it was certainly a very different problem to adopt such an attitude in the dark years of the war when Hitler's war machine was ruthlessly crushing all opposition, whether Jewish or Gentile. The Jews were not the only ones to be bestially murdered; French, Dutch and Czech villages were razed to the ground, and Poles and Russians were disposed of as if they were vermin. So that all in all, it is clear that Hitler and Hitlerism had no compunction in ruthlessly suppressing any opposition to their anti-racialist policies. The savage reprisals exacted upon the Dutch when they tried to protect the Jews is a case in point. Therefore, one understands why the Pope hesitated to take the plunge and to provoke another type of blood bath.

The fact is that protests were of no avail to Hitler and the Nazis, who never hesitated to deal with priests who opposed them. When in 1939, Poland was occupied by the Germans, the Poles themselves asked the Vatican to stop its campaign in their defence, on the plea that it made oppression worse. Numerous bishops and archbishops in Germany, Holland, Belgium, France and Poland protested in vain. The Pope joined them, approved of them, and gave explicit instructions that they should all do their best, according to their judgment, so as not to make things worse. He also gave repeated instructions to save the Jews, and large numbers were saved by Catholics in France, Hungary, Italy and elsewhere. The Israel Government, the Great Rabbi of Jerusalem and other Jewish organisations have publicly expressed their gratitude to the Pope and to the Catholic Church for what they had done for them during the war. This having been said, and bearing in mind the fact that Hitler had not waited for the war to do so, but had begun applying his violent anti-semitic policies as soon as he had achieved power through elections, to attempt to make the Pope partly or fully responsible for the crimes committed by Hitler and his acolytes upon the Jews, is neither commendably Christian nor matter for good drama.

When it comes to this very specific point, the purpose of the author is so obvious, and the means which he uses are so caricatural and biased that the result is no longer drama but

190

an indictment unsupported by evidence, and a melodramatic attempt at a so-called redemption of the guilt of the Pope and Papacy through the sacrifice of a rather presumptuous scapegoat whose size is all too clearly incommensurate with that of the Pope or of the Papacy. It is as incommensurate to them, in fact, as the death of Eichmann was for the crime of having killed six million Jews. Only a god could atone for such a super-human crime, just as only a saint could take upon himself to atone for the failure of Christ's Vicar on earth and for the Papacy. Ricardo's attempt to do so, without the slightest plausible ground for such claims looks like hollow conceit and is completely out of tune with the heart of Christian religion. Christ may have offered himself for the redemption of the sins of mankind, but Christ is not Moloch who accepts the sacrifice of priest or of any other human being in order to redeem the failings of another.

Therefore the claim to purify, for all eternity, the idea of the Papacy, is either pure and simple Satanism or mere inconsequential talk without any relevance to reality. In fact Ricardo shows a complete lack of Christian humility as when he boldly announces that he will pray for the salvation of the Pope as if God was entirely at his disposal. This type of arrogance turns into a strange perversion of the idea of God when Ricardo makes statements like: "How do we know that God is not sending a murderer to the Pope to save him from complete damnation", or "Judas knew he was damned to all Eternity. . . . His sacrifice was greater than that of God." * The idea of God as the murderer of the Pope in order to save his soul, or of God less aware than Judas, of the latter's fate and possible damnation is, to say the least, an extremely odd notion of Christianity, whether it is that of a Catholic priest like Ricardo or that of a Protestant writer, like the author. The idea of murdering the Pope, the High Priest, for the greater glory of God and His church on earth, might have been perfectly fitting with the tribal system of *The Golden Bough*, but it has never been part of Christianity, even in the days of the inquisition when priests and kings, angered by the

* The Representative, Methuen, p. 145.

Pope's unwillingness to play their own game, often enough wished that he would drop dead.

This very shaky theology, coupled with the fact that the author's hand is all too evidently at work, has resulted in cardboard-like characters sometimes made to move in a lurid background of snippets of filmed atrocities which make the presence of these characters even more unreal and incomprehensible, except in a few striking instances. The use of filmed extracts of concentration camps horrors, in a play which is not a true representation of reality but a subjective view of events and opinions, is a deceitful way of buttressing a tendentious thesis with emotionally charged facts. It is a process which seriously lets down the ethics of art, for it aims at making use of emotions roused by the sight of horrors, if not to blame the Pope for them, at least to blunt rational processes and make acceptable the author's thesis that the Pope has failed to prevent them through cowardice and Machiavellianism. This is an obvious lack of intellectual honesty which makes one long for the humility, profound humanity and sense of Christian responsibility so shiningly displayed by Pastor Niëmoller. The descriptions of the Pope and of his behaviour are not dispassionate, objective appraisals in which the dramatist carefully avoids taking sides, but on the contrary patterns of historical situations and characterisations which provoke the hatred of the author, and cannot therefore, fail to stir hatred against the Pope and against the Catholics who, according to the author, have behaved so inhumanly. One only has to remember Ricardo's description of the Pope* to realise that the heat which is generated is partly gratuitous, that it overflows the dramatic character, and that it can only be ascribed to a hatred of Papacy. "Hitler", says Ricardo, "will not alienate the Catholics of Europe for the sake of the Jews." The fact that most German Catholics were in Hitler's armies and, on the whole, doing what they were told, is glossed over. "We Germans are no worse than any other Europeans", says Gerstein. Very likely so! Anyway, few are those who would take up arms against

* The Representative, Methuen, p. 84.

192

this statement; on the other hand, very serious doubts and worry are raised when Gerstein continues with the words: "The conscience is a highly dubious seat of judgment, ... no, I seek an answer outside myself." O shades of Kant, for there lies the rub and the fateful flaw!—the readiness to obey orders, or, to blame others for orders given or for misdeeds which are supposed to be atoned for by scapegoats. Whatever one might think of the Pope's decision it cannot absolve individual responsibilities, yet the author obviously has striven hard in that direction and he has, by so doing, produced an extremely uneven play.

The first act, with the exception of some moments of unnecessary prolixity and confusion in the second scene, is good. After that, one plunges into the heart of the willed demonstration, and there, the incidents and brush strokes are clearly selected in order to produce the required picture. Of course, a dramatist is not a chronicler, and he has to select his facts; but, if he only selects those which give one side and one side only of an argument, he is no longer behaving as a dramatist but as a public prosecutor. There obviously are all sorts of cardinals, but in *The Representative* the only one we are shown is an effete, frivolous, snivelling caricature of a man who could only be used as a dramatic prop; if it had been offset by another type of prelate he would have contributed some complimentariness to this very lopsided picture. On the other hand, Ricardo is provided with wings and wisdom to such an immoderate degree that he often sounds like a prig. The third act is, on the whole, melodramatic and unnecessary. The fourth act, the encounter between Ricardo and the Pope which is obviously meant to be the climax of the play, is a failure, although of course Alan Webb, in the Aldwych production, gave a beautiful interpretation of the anxieties and hesitation of a conscience-stricken man, something which is certainly not part of the text. Far from it, the Pope is known under the derogatory label of "the chief", and he is given the full treatment. He is made to appear such a nincompoop that one wonders how such a man could ever hope to reach the level of a rural presbytery, least of all the holy see. As soon as he appears on the stage his overriding preoccupation is about his shares, and his anxiety is soon allayed by being presented with a cheque from American Jesuits who own aircraft factories in America. His main concern seems to be money from whatever source it might come, and the sources are, of course, evil. He not only thrives on armament shares from the Allies, he also sells mercury to Stalin who is a good customer of the Society of Jesus. Apart from his sordid gains, he is also worried that if factories were destroyed, the workers might become anarchists. Their suffering and their death of course do not matter in the least. All that matters is his obsession with communism which he is made to expound in a stupid tirade which concludes with a perfunctory exhortation to pray for the Jews. After that, Pilate-like, he is made to wash his hands in an attempt to clean away this indelible stain. This kind of simplicity might very well work in a nursery charade, but certainly not with adult audiences, and it is a pity that the author should have failed to see this, for the last act, which runs into sixty pages, is remarkably good, with the exception of the coda of the broadcast about the Pope's relations with Hitler, which is the required Q.E.D.

In fact the first and fifth acts, which are over a hundred pages long, together with some reporting about the Pope's and the Vatican's behaviour, would have been fully sufficient to make a good play. The evil doctor is particularly well drawn, and the scenes with Carlotta, Ricardo, Jacobson and Gerstein which are not scenes of exposition and theorising, as when the Pope is involved in them, but scenes of intense clash between living and deeply moving aspects of human personalities, are very good. They show true dramatic gifts, and it is therefore a pity that this last act was not shown in its entirety on the stage.

If the author had been able to forget about his anti-papism which is gratuitous and undramatic, and had concentrated his considerable dramatic powers and skill on the conflict of characters reasonably matched, he would have produced a very good play and not simply a dramatic work, often marred by melodramatic patches and hollow rhetoric used in order to expound a thesis. Indeed, whenever he endeavours to cut the Pope to size or to put forward claims that his own sacrifice could save the Church, Ricardo remains a rather presumptuous, unconvincing mouthpiece of the author. He only becomes dramatically effective in the scene with the evil doctor, that is to say, when he is totally divested from the sham apparel of a saint or of a symbol which he is not meant to wear, and when he confronts his own humanity and professed love of men with the daemonism of the doctor. The plight of Gerstein is just as moving, and if these men and women locked in conflict had not been compelled to involve themselves in ineffectual attempts to topple down with their bare hands and shouts the pyramid of the Church, they would have produced excellent drama. As it is, this play contains large desert stretches and much baying to the moon, which are neither pleasant nor rewarding. One can only wait for what Mr. Hochhuth will do next!

CHAPTER NINE

VIOLENCE, CRUELTY AND "THE THEATRE OF CRUELTY"

VIOLENCE and cruelty are not two interchangeable, synonymous terms. They imply on the contrary quite different notions. Violence is an instinctive reaction which is part of life. The animal world is naturally violent, because it is intent upon the gratification of its own instincts, but it is not cruel. A cat playing with a mouse is not being cruel but merely perfecting the mechanism which enables him to catch mice and to enjoy the game of catching them. Cruelty is specifically human, and whether it is cruelty to others as in sadism or cruelty to oneself as in masochism, it is irretrievably bound up with consciousness of self—a notion which pre-eminently distinguishes man from the animal. Delacroix's painting of a lion devouring a horse expresses at its best the natural ferocity and violence of the animal world. The lion is a perfect machine carrying out its purpose, and the objective and detached way in which the scene is described indicates a purely phenomenal approach to the theme which the painter handles. In this case, he does not comment, he merely observes and describes. Michelangelo does the same in his battle scenes sketches in which the violence is merely muscular, without any suggestion of cruelty. The battle scenes of Da Vinci partake of the same, purely muscular violence. The agonised look, the tormented agony of suffering only come in with religious subjects and they show that cruelty is only possible in a religious background as a form of sadism and as a denial of the idea of God or of the sacredness of the individual self.

The violence of the Greek world was an integral part of life. Christ had not yet come to earth, and men, ruled by fate and by capricious gods, inflicted violent death, without qualms, knowing full well that their turn would come. Achilles turned a deaf ear to Hector's plea for mercy, knowing that he himself would get none. Icarus, in Breughel's picture, disappears into the sea without causing the slightest distraction to the ploughman near by who continues unmoved the ploughing of his field. The violence of Greek tragedy takes place in a religious context, a context in which death was a necessary means of purgation and redemption. Oedipus has to get rid of eyes which did not prevent him from committing parricide and incest, and he has to die in order that the gods' wrath against his sinful family might at last be placated and that his remains might acquire numinous properties.

The great Greek tragedies are symbolic entities embodying archetypal messages and religious rites, in a similar way in which the mass is a religious ritual. They are, in every respect, completely non-naturalistic. Their main characters are all legendary and heroic figures which could not fit in any naturalistic context; therefore the truth of their actions is never literal, naturalistic or directly social, but always symbolic and imaginative, that is to say transcending the contingent. The theocentric medieval world was dominated by philosophic realism, that is to say by the belief that every part of creation had existence and was informed with the subsistent cause which gave it life. Therefore, every aspect of creation was part of God's world and the artist who could describe it with exactitude could bring out the thisness or the being of the thing which he described. This was phenomenalism before this form of thought was systematised. Villon's picture of *La Belle Heaumière* is an accurate, totally objective description of the decay of old age, without the slightest attempt at comments which are part of conceptualism. In such a climate, the passion plays were produced with such stark realism that they were really a re-enactment of the suffering of Christ or of the martyrs whose actions were portrayed on the stage. These portrayals, which were part of religious ritual, were means of stimulating the faith and of atoning for the sins shared by all men and which had caused

Christ's or the martyrs' suffering. They were part of a world united by, and individually and continuously connected with, God's laws. They were like hair-shirts, bare feet pilgrimages and fasts, tokens of sympathy for Christ's suffering and deeds of atonement. Suffering was an integral part of life and it was neither sadistic nor conceptual. These aspects of suffering came later, with the eighteenth and nineteenth centuries and they have reached their full scope with the twentieth.

Leaving out the religious background which during the Renaissance had broken down and is never explicitly stated in Shakespeare's tragedies these tragedies are, irrespective of the social and historical elements which they necessarily carry, essentially symbolic entities which cannot be interpreted naturalistically without being considerably scaled down and transformed into something which they are not. *Othello* can no more be reduced to the level of a "crime passionel" than *Phèdre* and *Hamlet* can be reduced to that of psychiatric cases. One can read into these plays which are so fully universal as to contain practically every aspect of human behaviour, any kind of social and historical analogy which is uppermost at a given moment or in a given mind, but to reduce them to a limited, social and time-marked aspect, is to detract seriously from their greatness and to use them as means for the propagation or the buttressing of given beliefs. Historical situations are each unique; therefore all historical transpositions are false. There are similarities of attributes, facts and events, there are no total repetitions or absolute identities.

The violence of Othello is mostly sacramental and is intent upon destruction in order to purify. The violence of the world of Lear cannot be equated with that of our own world. It is the violence of chaos let loose and of ruthless individualism run wild. This violence is unleashed by a gesture which mirrors the irresponsible and utterly selfish repudiation of the natural order, which, though this is not mentioned, could also be the Divine order. Things have fallen apart, the centre is no longer there. That does not mean that when there was a centre there was no violence. Far from it; there was plenty of violence such as religious wars and crusades, but it was of a different nature, for violence though endemic to mankind, can have many causes. Lear can no more be reduced to the level of a plain, testy old man (and plain is the operative word) than Hamlet can be turned into an angry, dissatisfied young man. The former could not be made to look like Archie Rice's father, and the latter could not be placed behind a sweets stall in the Midlands. Lear and Hamlet are archetypal characters whose actions are prisms through which large sections of mankind can, at all times, see aspects of their own behaviour, thoughts and affectivity. They do not specifically mirror the Kentish or Danish society of their day or of Shakespeare's days, they mirror man *sub specie aeternitatis*.

Hamlet's discontent with the world is as cosmic as the irresponsibility of Lear, and they are both part of organically built symbolic structures in which all details are subsumed into a whole, so that their respective value is never contingent or intrinsic but always related to this whole. If one looks at these details in such a light one can see a vast difference between the gouging out of Gloucester's eyes and the cruelty of concentration camps or the ritual murders of modern plays. The cruelty inflicted upon Gloucester is both practically real and also symbolical. The truth of such a deed does not lie in itself but in what it stands for; yet of course in order to be able to stand for something, it must have first and foremost all the attributes of realistic truth. This is obviously the kind of behaviour which was part and parcel of Shakespeare's world in which deeds like cutting off tongues or hands and gouging out of eyes were still part of a pattern of a rough and ready code of primitive justice. But the realistic truth embodied in such a deed is, in this case as in all Shakespeare's great plays, only a grain or a sign used for the building up of the transcending symbolic truth of the play. Blindness has descended upon Lear's world, and Gloucester needs no more his eyes to discover the truth, than Lear needs his reason to determine his behaviour; so, one has to grope through blindness and the other through madness, for the truth which they have both lost.

199

The violence of the Shakespearian and Racinian world is the violence of a tragic world, a world which implies conflict between heroic, superhuman characters (essentially non-naturalistic) and forces which overwhelm them and over which they can only triumph through death. The actions which these characters go through are presented, as befits them and the vision of the poet who creates them, in a language which is always used both as a means to convey meaning and to make an entity which exists, not as the mere sum of its component parts or aspects, but as a whole which alone determines the meaning which can be ascribed to the various parts and aspects which go to its making. Even *Othello*, which carries a greater load of psychological motivation and dramatic tension than any one of the other great tragedies, shows a hero marked from the beginning for his catastrophic downfall. Although *Phèdre* carries evident traces of the age in which it was written, Phèdre herself is caught, from the beginning, in forces which are as much beyond her control as those which swept Oedipus to his death. Whether or not these motivations contain an admixture of Jansenism and psychological truth, they operate in a religious background, and their unfolding, imaginatively perceived, embodies the very plight of all those who now and always, are swept by passions which they cannot master.

The violence of tragedy is a violence which is neither social nor gratuitous or sadistic, but part of the means to restore the temporarily disrupted poetic justice of a timeless world. This violence has been given a style which excludes any possible naturalistic interpretation and it has been clothed into a perfectly controlled form which, excluding the mimetism of naturalism, objectifies the whole. Racine's fierce passions, Shakespeare's great flights of imagination are fused into polished, perfectly orchestrated verse so that the blend between Dionysian intoxication and Apollonian control—the dream of great art—is achieved. Some great romantic artists like Delacroix, Goethe and Hölderlin, who looked upon violence as being inherent to the human make-up, sought to impose upon it the same formal Apollonian control.

Both Ibsen and Strindberg deal at times with violence in naturalistic settings but when they do so, as is the case with *Miss Julie* for instance, they do so within one single context, without any admixture of genres and styles and in a self-contained world explored to its depth. When Ibsen or Strindberg want to enlarge their meaning and reach out for symbolic violence they carefully build up their own universe in which symbolism and realism form a whole in which the truths expressed have perennial value. *Rosmersholm, The Master Builder, Brand* are plays which illustrate this approach to dramatic truth. Violence in a naturalistic context must be justified by the situation and by the nature of the characters involved, and, in order to be credible, it must appear as the natural, unavoidable outcome of the situation and of the characters, as is the case in *Miss Julie*. One cannot pass from naturalistic to symbolic and ritualistic meanings, for such juxtapositions merely produce conceptual constructions and not works of imagination. In the same way, a tragedy is not a matter of a death or deaths but of climate and of the causes which led to them. The Maid's words at the end of *Victor* by Vitrac: "It's a tragedy", does not alter the fact that the three bodies littered about the bedroom are part of a farce, and a good one too, and not of a tragedy. Violence in naturalistic situations often calls forth, not imaginative experience, but kinetic reactions of loathing or approval in a subjective and not, as it should in true art, in an objective way.

The violence of our age, the sadistic violence of concentration camps, or the gratuitous violence of bored youth which is portrayed in some modern works, is part of the cult of sensualism and conceptualism which is characteristic of the age. Now, "to feel is to exist", and through strong sensations, to assert one's power and one's own egoism, together with the total negation of the other. The suffering which is portrayed on the stage nowadays is sometimes cathartic and sometimes, alas, only part of the desire to indulge the love of sensations of the age, therefore part of the drug which one swallows, or the lies which one invents in order to avoid facing the reality of truth.

Naturalistic violence is irreconcilable with the idea of the theatre of cruelty which is quite in fashion now. Antonin Artaud, the originator of this rather vague, catchy tag was explicit beyond any doubt on this point. "My inclinations are for a theatre . . . which turns its back on life and on the real, and admits no limits or visible transpositions, a theatre not based on the usual psychology of human characters . . . in brief, a theatre in which the mind completely free can expand in all its forms. . . . This theatre would bring back to the public the notion of the absolute spectacle and would be the equivalent of an intellectual music-hall in which all the senses and all the faculties of the mind would be satisfied. . . . The most difficult would be to find plays; but Hölderlin's *Empedocles*, Shelley's *Cenci*, a play by Byron the *Revengeur's Tragedy*, etc. would be part of the programme."* To this list of plays he added *Arden of Feversham*, *The Duchess of Malfi*, *The White Devil*, a play by De Sade, and the much talked about and fashionable *Woyzeck*. Not a single play by Shakespeare, Racine or any one of the great masters was included in the list of his productions. "The point upon which I insist", he said, "is that the plays I have chosen are not for me an end but a means; they are such as not to hinder the staging processes which I have in mind."† One could not be more outspoken in one's disregard for the intrinsic value of a play, and one could not, of course, offer greater causes for praise in an age when the producer dominates the theatre.

"Those who wish to give back to the public its faith in the theatre, and specially in a certain literary theatre with consecrated works—Aeschylus, Euripides, Shakespeare, Molière, Corneille, Racine simply spit by the side of the spittoon; these writers' works being a dead language, which, Aeschylus excluded . . . could offer no real interest." What Antonin Artaud wanted was pretexts for staging and nothing else. "I intend to try to build up, around a well-known theme —popular or sacred—one or many theatrical realisations in which gestures, attitudes and signs will be improvised while

* Letter to J. R. Bloch, 23 April 1931.
† Letter to Dalio, 27 June 1932.

they are thought out, directly on the stage, and the words will come as a conclusion in order to reach the known domain of lyrical discourse composed of music, gestures and living signs."* In an article published by *Paris Soir*, 14 July 1932, and entitled "The Theatre which I wish to create", Artaud sought to define his aims. "My idea of the theatre is something religious and metaphysical in the sense of a truly magic, real and totally effective action. I give to the words 'religion' and 'metaphysical' a meaning which has nothing to do with religion or metaphysics in their usual sense. . . . The problem I wish to solve is that of allowing the theatre to find again its true language—a language of space, of gestures, attitudes, expressions and mimicry, a language of cries and onomato-poeias, a language of sounds, a language in which all these objective elements will become signs which, whether visual or auditive, will have as great an intellectual importance and apprehensible meaning as a language embodied in words, for words are by now employed only for the discursive and arrested aspects of life." One can see at once the vitalising aspects of some of Artaud's proposed reforms in the theatre, and also the utter confusion and the shallowness of some of his notions. If gestures, music, sound and lighting are rightly recognised as necessary in order to make of the theatrical performance an experience which involves the totality of the human person, they had not been discovered by Artaud. Gordon Craig, Appia, and to a certain extent Copeau, had already stressed to the limits the importance of lighting, physical gestures and music; yet all these contributory elements cannot take the place of the words, and "give birth to works as beautiful as those in any language", as Artaud suggests, or carry sustained and complex meanings. Gestures, mimicry, movements and music can convey emotions, feelings and experiences, but cannot take the place of the words. Verdi's *Othello* and *Macbeth* are not Shakespeare's *Othello* and *Macbeth*; they are very different both in range and in emotional and intellectual complexity, and the advantage clearly remains with the dramatist.

* Letter to Van Caulaert, 5 July 1932.

Artaud was more intent in producing spectacles than in producing plays. There is, naturally, room for both forms of entertainment and what is more, there is room for a marriage of both, for a play is a spectacle; yet a great play can no more be made to disappear in the spectacle than a great actor or actress can be turned into a mere instrument in the producer's hands. Yet such was Artaud's aim: "What is called the personality of the actor must disappear. . . . In the theatre the actor as actor can no longer be allowed to have the slightest initiative."* This is perhaps possible with mediocre, second-rate actors, but certainly not with actors like Gielgud, Olivier or Scofield and actresses like Dame Edith Evans or any performer of a similar stature. A great actor is endowed with the gift of negative capability, that is to say, with the gift of being whatever character he sets about to give scenic existence. The character which he portrays is not a projection of his own personality, except in cases of failure or innate limitations, but a blend of his personality with that prompted by the work of the author with whom he is collaborating in order to give existence in time and space to an imaginary character.

No producer, unless he is also a great actor, can possibly claim to be able to feel himself into the inner structure of a great dramatic character, with the intuitive certainties of a great actor. The latter may, if left to himself, unbalance the play or impose upon it a slant which the detached, objective eye of the producer could correct, but if the play which is being produced is a great play, no amount of good team work and skill in production can compensate for the absence of a great actor, endowed with the capability of rising to the heights of the part.

Artaud was first and foremost concerned with the demiurgic powers of the producer. His ideal medium should have been the cinema and not the theatre, for there he would have been in a position to submit everything and everyone to his will. The film actor's primary aim being sincerity, improvisation, spontaneity and method training in the art of exteriorising emotions through gestures and movements are all part of his

---

* Letter to G. Gallimard, 11 August 1932.

technique for achieving it. He has, besides that, the camera's invaluable help and the possibility of concentrating on isolated scenes which he can repeat over and over again. The stage actor can neither improvise his part every night, nor go through it in isolated sections. He must have both an intuitive and intellectual grasp of the character he is portraying, and, at best, an all-embracing grasp of the play. His aim is not to be sincere, but to compose a picture or an appearance, from which the audience will apprehend the character he is portraying. He has no camera to show his tears or the twitching of his skin, so he must find the gesture, the movement and the tone of voice which will make clear to the audience the state he is in. In order to be able to do that, he must be a highly individualised and gifted performer, and not a mechanical instrument in the hands of a producer.

When we come to Artaud's notion of "the theatre of cruelty", we find that this formula was merely a catch phrase, a journalistic headline. Actors and plays were, for him, only cogs in the spectacular machine which he wished to build up. What he sought, above all, was the gratification of his own rather overdeveloped ego which certainly did not suffer from modesty. He was devoured by revolutionary passion, and harassed as he was by material and moral difficulties, his frenzied mind made him flail about with great vigour and also with a general lack of discrimination, against any impediment which he wished to dispose of. He explained that he was operating in the field of pure ideas and metaphysics "without taking into account any human nuances which could only hamper me and paralyse my actions". The theatre is an existential art and not a mystical mediation or a fakir's levitation above the earth. It is indeed made of human nuances and complexities which cannot be conveyed through puppetry, balletics and *Son et Lumière* effects. Artaud was obviously not always sure of the boundaries between the real and the imaginary, and while there is food for thought in his writings, there is also food for indigestion and flatulence. His much-discussed "theatre of cruelty" is a case in point. "I have chosen as a title 'theatre of cruelty' . . . for the following reasons: the real title would be too vast and impossible to formulate—it should be 'alchemical or metaphysical theatre' that would be a vast joke for those who are not informed. There is no successful spectacle without an element of cruelty, the important point is the use which the spectacle makes of this cruelty which is a kind of cosmic cruelty, a near relation of the destruction without which nothing can be created. That is the meaning of the title as I explain it in the manifesto. That is enough for us, and I think it will be an attraction for the public. . . . If you have another title, please let me have it, or, put it at the top of the printed text on your own authority."* Writing again to Paulhan, in September of the same year, he said "the aim is to give to the theatrical spectacle the appearance of a devouring fire and to bring at least once in the course of it, the action, the structure of the play and its images, to the degree of implacable incandescence which, in the psychological or cosmic domain, is identified with cruelty."

Writing to André Gide (20 August 1932) he said " I ask you to allow me to announce that you intend to write a play for the theatre which I should call *The Theatre of Cruelty*, and that you will do so, starting from the stage and in liaison with the staging. I shall announce it at the head of the list of the spectacles which I propose to stage and which are:

(1) An extract from the Zohar, the story of Rabbi Ben Simeon who burns like fire.

(2) The capture of Jerusalem with the blood red colour which flows from it. . . .

(3) The story of Blue Beard according to the archives and with new ideas about eroticism and cruelty.

(4) A story by the Marquis de Sade, in which eroticism will be transposed, represented erotically and presented as a violent exteriorisation of cruelty.

(5) One or many romantic melodramas in which the improbable will become an active and strong element in poetry.

(6) Woyzeck by Buckner, as a reaction against my prin-

* Letter to Jean Paulhan, 29 August 1932.

ciples, and in order to show what can be done with a coherent and precise text.

(7) Works from the Elizabethan theatre shorn of their text, from which I shall only retain the characters, the climate of the time, the situations and naturally the action."

With this list in mind, one easily understands the now quite widespread notion that poetry is an improbability or an adornment which requires to be discarded in order to reach the truth, the not infrequent attempts to reduce Shakespeare's plays to elemental and topical actions, and the attempt made in order to give cruelty and violence the same cosmic importance which Freud gave to sex, that is to say an importance totally out of proportion with the truth. The much talked about De Sade was fully engrossed in the satisfaction of his own sexual pleasures which oscillated between perversity, sadism and masochism. The "other", was for him an object for the gratification of his sensual pursuits. His revolutionary ideas did not transcend his selfishness, and his anarchism did not exclude the social order from which he extracted whatever he could, before society paid him back in his own money. The De Sades of this world are only exceptions, and though real and significant, they should neither claim nor be given all the attention of humankind.

NOTE. Michelangelo's dying captives and his risen Christ have the serenity of face and beauty of body of his David. It is only with the Rondanina and other Pietas that we have the intense sorrow and physical exhaustion which seems to lift bodies from the earth into the pure world of spirit. Da Vinci moves in a world of effortless grace, plastic muscularity and empyrean beauty untouched by the distortions and spiritual fervour of Gothicism. Bellini's St. Sebastian stands by the side of the Holy Trinity, with an arrow stuck in his entrails and looking no more perturbed than if it were a fly on his skin.

CHAPTER TEN

CONCLUDING REMARKS

LANDMARKS must not be confused with scaffoldings; landmarks are what they are. An observer can only use them as means of orientation, or as significant features of a given landscape. He cannot draw them to himself or use them for his own ends, he can only describe their phenomenal appearance so as to suggest the essence or nature of the landscape to which they belong. A scaffolding is always something man-made, something prepared for a purpose which is to support a construction or conclusions. It is a structure for a demonstration, a thesis, or an oration, that is to say, it is the expression of a form of rhetoric aimed at carrying conviction; it therefore implies a kind of intentionality alien to art which presupposes disinterestedness, unconceptualised interplay of all the forms which belong to a given theme, or, pure phenomenalism in criticism.

A great writer is obviously a landmark, but one who is a landmark is not necessarily a great or a major writer. Edgar Poe is by no stretch of imagination a great writer, yet he undeniably is a landmark in the sense that he crystallises in himself certain definite aspects of middle nineteenth-century sensibility, something which caused him to have a notable influence on his age and beyond. Goethe and Baudelaire are both great poets and great landmarks. Claudel is at the same time a major poet and an important landmark, yet in spite of the variety and magnitude of his achievements, he has neither reached the impact and universality of Baudelaire's limited output, nor given to the sensibility of his age, the range of consciousness and expression which have made Baudelaire's work so vital and influential that it has taken three major poets—Yeats, Claudel and Eliot to achieve a similar scope.

The aim of this study precludes the drawing up of conclusions which have by no means been posited by a prepared
structure. The landmarks described are part of a common
landscape, that is to say part of a changing pattern which is an
unfolding historical moment. As such, one can know some of
its characteristics, but one cannot know what it really is,
since such a moment has not yet passed from the state of living
to the state of destiny or object. One cannot, for instance,
know it in the way one knows the Classical or the Romantic
moment, in which light and shadows, heights and hollows,
beauty and ugliness have by now found their more or less
unchanging level into a recognisable picture, the perspective
and the general impression of which only slightly vary with
the changing position of the viewer. One could of course, even
in this case, be given Bishop Berkeley's answer that "to be is
to be perceived", that there are no things in themselves, and
that there is only the apprehension and the use which human
consciousness makes of them for its project. Historical facts,
and above all events, are of that nature; they are always part
of the project of the consciousness which illumines them and
dredges them up from the dark where countless others cease-
lessly fade into nothingness. The more remote in time facts,
events and lives are, the greater the core of thingness which
makes for greater objectivity. None of the writers examined
here falls in this category. They are all very much alive, even
the dead, therefore none can be assessed with finality. Yet,
although the living continue to develop and to change, their
changes are, up to a point, limited by their past, and on the
whole, the longer the past, the narrower the scope of change
in the future. Each writer can only express certain structures
of his genius, which determine his themes, his inner music
and the range of his colours. If he has no genius and only
talent, he is free to adapt himself to the changing moods and
needs of the time and society in which he lives and which he
might try to satisfy. Yet, the fundamental aim of art is not to
satisfy society but to reveal to it what it truly is.

If one cannot predict what a writer will do, one can at
least put forward probabilities and discard possibilities. It is

obvious, for instance, that Beckett will write neither *Mother Courage* nor *Chicken Soup with Barley*. The bent of his genius and the bases of his main themes are by now so clearly set as to preclude any move in these directions. He could only attempt to do so if he felt that this was the only way to success; and that would be something completely alien to someone whose singlemindedness and uncompromising honesty are part of his poetic genius. He might possibly have attempted such explorations if he had been unaware of the nature of his creativeness, but again, he is too mature and too conscious of his inner truths to still carry in himself such patches of obscurity about his true capabilities. The road between *Waiting for Godot, Endgame* and *Play* might be long, but the climate and the landscape along which it runs have not changed much. Trees have disappeared, physical agitation has been reduced to the bare minimum, legs no longer move but twitch, yet we are still in the same bleak world on the edge of doom.

Miller, Tennessee Williams, Edward Albee, Pinter and Wesker seem to have remained throughout, identical to themselves, while they each continue to explore, with varying degrees of success, the themes which they have made their own. John Osborne and Robert Bolt have both proved that they could successfully enlarge their range by being careful not to work beyond their possibilities. Although *Luther* is an historical play, it still carries with it a good deal of the irritation against the established order which is found in *Look Back in Anger. A Man for all Seasons* is Bolt's best play. John Arden has also endeavoured to widen his range and he has shown that he is at his best with themes which enable him to use his poetic imagination and his remarkable command of language. On the other hand, Peter Shaffer who has made a similar attempt, has shown, alas, that he is most deficient in these two qualities. His play: *Five Finger Exercise* was an excellent piece of naturalistic and probably autobiographical cannibalism which had a well-deserved success. His attempt at epic drama with the *Royal Hunt of the Sun* has laid bare a certain shallowness of ideas, lack of characterising powers

and the failure of his pseudo-poetical language. His hero—
Pizarro, a hollow husk of a character, saddled with too many
queries and unsolved topical questions—shambles through
the play, only coming partly alive after two hours of inter-
mittent boredom. Deprived of either historical or human
truth, supposedly caught in a conflict between two civiliza-
tions, which never truly materialises, he is never moving
enough to awaken sympathy or interest. To complete it all,
the parodic crucifixion of the thirty-three-year-old Inca king,
taken down from his stake, Christ like, shows a lack of sensibility, which neither a masterly production nor some good
moments could redeem.

In France, Billetdoux is the only noteworthy dramatist to
have moved successfully from his first naturalistic play—
Tchin-Tchin, through the more ambiguous and complex
Va-t-en Chez Thorpe, to his essay in Brechtianism and balletics of his latest and quite successful play—*Comment va le
Monde Mossieu*. Ionesco continues to be Ionesco, a blend of
naturalism and fantasy, not a landmark but a kind of antheap
raised by fashion and avant gardism, which is likely to subside
to its true proportions in due course. The most interesting
playwright to have recently appeared on the French stage is
Spanish-born, French-writing, Fernando Arrabal. His one-act
play, *Picnic on the Battlefield*, is a humorous fantastic exploration of the theme of war, showing the gullibility and simple-
mindedness of common people who are the tools of their
exploiters who involve them in wars in which friends and
foes are destroyed by the blind forces of war. Stretcher-bearers,
as simple-minded as the soldiers they are supposed to minister
to, find in this hecatomb the opportunity of carrying out
their set task and an unreasoned source of satisfaction which
will be probably terminated by the next random load of
bombs. Absurd, all this certainly is, if one looks at it from the
moon, but it certainly is not so, if one thinks that it is men
who do such things to other men! And if one thinks so, one
might feel compelled to forget about this detergent-like epithet
which washes everything to the same neutral whiteness, and
one might get down to seeing what can be done to deal with

men and a society which permit such inhuman cruelty. The *Car Cemetery* is a moving, sad farce, set in a junkyard of old cars, in which a Christ-like musician, a charitable prostitute, an impeccable waiter and other odd specimens of human kind, single-mindedly engrossed in their individual pursuits, show the remarkable versatility of the author's talents. Another of Arrabal's plays, *Fando and Lis*, is a heartrending mixture of compulsive cruelty and devotion to unattainable ideals and to a person who is destroyed in the process. These three plays show that their author has talents well beyond the range of some who hold the stage now.

The great artistic lights of the contemporary world are still Picasso, Klee, Kandinski, Kokoshka, Braque, Rouault, Matisse, Henry Moore, Barbara Hepworth, Stravinsky, Claudel, Yeats, O'Neill, Brecht, Eliot, Kafka, Sartre, Malraux and William Faulkner, all transmuters of reality into imaginative entities which are crystals through which mankind, whatever colour and creed, can find facets of its own image. All these artists are concerned with the true reality which imagination reveals. Naturalism, which is to truth what photography is to great painting, is always a sectional, composite aspect of phenomenal reality and never an organic synthesis created by imagination. The camera, however skilfully it may be guided by heart and mind, and whatever the theme and aim pursued, can only use percepts and fragments of percepts in order to compose a picture. The painter sieves these percepts through years of subconscious processings which extract from them essences which blend with others to create new forms made to emerge from the dark into new objects which the artist only recognises as such once he has created them. He could neither analyse the details of their component parts, nor recreate them, for he has no conceptual mould of them. On the other hand, with naturalism and photography, the concept is the dominant element.

Social realism, a group of words which implies a blatant misuse of the word realism, means really conformity to socialism, that is to say conformity to ideology, but certainly not to reality. Social realism aims at representing, not objective reality, but the changing reality of a revolutionary society. The artist in that society must always depict society in the light of what he thinks that tomorrow will be. This tomorrow is determined by dogmatic creeds to which he must sacrifice his freedom, for "he must", as Zhadanov, the expounder of the creed has said, "submit the truth and the historicity of his creations to the purpose of educating and transforming the ideology of the workers in conformity with the spirit of socialism". The world certainly seems to move towards socialism, but it is unlikely to be the socialism of militant China, or even that of Russia, however much Russian political wisdom may have humanely altered in search of this goal. The artist who did not conform to the canons of the socialist society was, until recently, either imprisoned, banned or ostracised as was the case with Pasternak. Yet, one can train a lion or an elephant to stand on his hind legs, one can lead talent to perform whatever gesture the state may require, but one cannot reconcile genius with external directives or willed political and religious aims, for genius is the unfettered expression, according to its own inner laws and structures, of the subterranean forces of an age and of history itself.

Whether we accept or not the notion that we move towards socialism, the essence of art is neither to prove nor to preach the veracity and necessity of such a belief, but to express impartially the various forces which struggle to foster or to hamper it. These forces are embodied into symbolic entities which in literature are composed of imagination-born individuals whose thoughts, feelings and actions illumine experience, enlarge the field of human consciousness, and therefore increase the spiritualisation of man. This cannot be attained by edicts from Zhadanovs or any other Government agencies. Brecht, who knew exactly what social realism meant, eluded the stifling embrace of Moscow or East Berlin, by skilful ambiguities. He only sacrificed to this creed in his theories and sometimes in plays which are already anachronistic.

A concomitant notion to that of naturalism and Social realism is that which sees in poetry an adornment of speech or a means of felicitously conveying ideas. Those who entertain such notions look upon poetic plays, including Shakespeare's, as leafy worlds from which they must extract meanings which they generally emphasise to the detriment of the whole. A play of *Hamlet*'s or *Lear*'s magnitude is a prism which can offer each generation various aspects of itself; but to fasten on one single facet or to stress one or two given aspects only of naturalistic truth, is obviously to scale down these plays and to reduce them to being mirrors of the thoughts and beliefs which prevail at a given moment or in certain persons. Hamlet's complexities can no more be reduced to one single meaning than the Gioconda's smile. They are both embodiments of the blend of realism, mystery and intellectual awakening which forms the texture of the age to which they belong. Poetic language is a way of giving life to thoughts and feelings which cannot be decomposed into content and expression without impoverishment. A poet does not first conceive in prose something which he later clothes in poetry; he creates in poetry a living, organic entity which cannot be neatly decomposed into characters, meanings and social problems, without being destroyed. That our age of prose is no longer used to poetry as the main medium of expression is a well-established and fully accepted fact which militates against any form of poetic drama. Strict, orthodox versification has been repudiated; although, of course, poetic language is no more confined to verse than poetic drama is confined to elevated subjects and speech. *The Family Reunion*, *Waiting for Godot*, *Marching Song*, *Sergeant Musgrave's Dance*, to quote only a few, dispose of this kind of notion. Poetry is part of all aspects of life, and profound emotions and tense situations organise themselves in rhythmic and poetry charged language which conveys more than what it can say logically. O'Neill's language sometimes rises above stylistic weaknesses on the wings of poetic imagination. In the same way, Pinter's moves from naturalistic speech to the rich and complex music of poetry. Poetry is neither the cream on the bun, nor flights of fancy and hollow, tinselly images; it is above all, precision of images and metaphors and continuous contact with reality through imagination. When the contact with reality is lost, it is fancy which is part of comedy but not of serious drama.

In prose, words are stills of sensations and thoughts and signs which lead to the signified thing and then disappear once they have reached it. In poetry, the words are the incarnation of a reality or of an imaginative experience which is an organic whole endowed with the fluidity and the continuous creativeness of the dance. If the language of poetic drama were only used to convey ideas and logical meanings, then any good translation which does just that would be as good as, if not better than, the original, since it would have stripped the text to its bare sinews of rational communication. Yet, a mere reading or watching of a performance of *Hamlet* in Gide's perfectly accurate prose-translation, will at once make clear the shortcomings of such an approach to the play and the aspects of the play which it generally throws into relief. Language purely used as a means of a communication tends to put the emphasis upon action, movement and social characterisation, to the detriment of the atmosphere of brooding forces, mystery and archetypal grandeur which generally dominate tragedy. Hamlet, in this case, sheds part of his perplexities and agonising doubts carefully embodied in a language which expresses his complex poetic being, to become a more intellectual, more extrovert, and more limited Renaissance prince whose aptitudes for action could, with a spot of luck, have rendered unnecessary the accession to the throne of the true man of action, Fortinbras. All these things are as much part of the text as they were part of the age when the play was written, an age of action, extrovertness and intellectual ebullience, together with great changes in political and religious thinking and structures. Although in our time there is again a good deal of worshipping of the intellect, there is no sufficient reason to overemphasise one or two aspects of great works to the detriment of their wholeness which has perennial validity. It is not because we are living in an age of socialism that we should compel Shakespeare to join the socialist party, to echo the post-Nietzschean night of the death of God with the cry of "absurdity", or to shout "down with the colour bar"!

INDEX

Index